LEEDS CITY COLLEGE
SOUTH LEEDS CENTRE LIBRARY

brilliant **job**

brilliant job hunter's manual

your complete guide to getting the job you want

Angela Fagan

 Prentice Hall
FINANCIAL TIMES

An imprint of **Pearson Education**
Harlow, England • London • New York • Boston • San Francisco • Toronto
Sydney • Tokyo • Singapore • Hong Kong • Seoul • Taipei • New Delhi
Cape Town • Madrid • Mexico City • Amsterdam • Munich • Paris • Milan

PEARSON EDUCATION LIMITED

Edinburgh Gate
Harlow CM20 2JE
Tel: +44 (0)1279 623623
Fax: +44 (0)1279 431059
www.pearsoned.co.uk

First published in Great Britain in 2003

ISBN 10: 0-273-66315-1
ISBN 13: 978-0-273-66315-7

British Library Cataloguing in Publication Data
A CIP catalogue record for this book can be obtained from the British Library.

10 9 8

Designed by Claire Brodmann Book Designs, Lichfield, Staffordshire
Typeset by Northern Phototypesetting Co Ltd, Bolton
Printed and bound in Great Britain by Bell & Bain Ltd., Glasgow

The Publishers' policy is to use paper manufactured from sustainable forests.

Contents

Introduction

So what's different about this book?

During my career in the UK recruitment industry I regularly encountered job hunters who had no clear idea where they were going in their career and had a very limited knowledge of the techniques of job hunting. This is hardly surprising since it is something that we are expected to understand and to be able to do, but who do you learn from?

In my role as a recruitment consultant I was in a position to offer advice and counselling to individuals who crossed the doors of my agency, but what help did everyone else out there get? Surely there must be a book that I could recommend to people that they could buy? A book that would provide them with a comprehensive guide to everything they wanted to know about getting the job they wanted.

I looked at many different publications and found that they concentrated on only one or two parts of the job search, were heavily biased towards an American audience or, more importantly, were written by individuals who had little in common with the majority of job hunters today.

I came across many job hunters who had been stuck in a job they disliked for many years and had put up with it because they thought it was the best they could get. Paralysed by the fear of moving jobs, they had allowed themselves to become unhappy and to let events control them, instead of taking control.

I hope to provide inspiration not only to the unhappy employee but also to the first-time job hunter and individuals who find themselves out of a job due to redundancy or dismissal. You all come with the same hopes, fears and aspirations. I aim to tackle all of these issues in this book, enabling you to feel empowered and in control of your life and career.

I set out with the task of drawing together all my experience in the recruitment market with my knowledge of the way this industry really works, to compile a book which would arm you, the job hunter, with as much information and advice as possible to go out there confidently and get the job you want.

The book covers: analysis of your needs as an individual, identifying the type of job you want, where to look for that job, compiling your CV and performing well at interviews. Presented warts and all in an easy-to-follow format, no more jargon, just honest, straightforward advice.

We will also take a look at the role of recruitment consultants to enable you really to understand what they do and how they can help you, as well as tackling some common misconceptions.

The power of the internet in job hunting goes from strength to strength every year. Over 50% of UK households now have access and it is rapidly becoming the preferred medium for employers advertising jobs. I have compiled a listing of over 300 job sites specifically targeting the UK market, presented in an easy-to-read format identifying their coverage and specialisation. Find the information you need quickly and easily by market sector, no more spending hours online trying to locate the job site that is right for you.

I have also included a listing of every major UK national and local newspaper together with their web addresses to help you to identify the best publication to help you find the job for you.

You will learn how to:

■ identify what you really want from a job

■ compile a knockout CV to gain an advantage over your fellow job hunters

■ get the best out of recruitment consultants

■ do well during telephone interviews and assessment centres

■ understand psychometric testing

■ put in a great performance at interviews with guidance on over 50 of the most common questions and suggested answers

■ negotiate a job offer

■ deal with rejection.

part one

where to
start

'Minds are like parachutes – they only function when open.'

Thomas Dewar

1 What to consider

Making the decision to move

Moving jobs can be one of the most stressful situations we encounter; it ranks high up there with divorce and moving house. Our fulfilment levels of life are closely linked with what job we do and, more importantly, whether we enjoy that job.

Through our jobs we often meet our partners and develop lifelong friends; while our knowledge base is being expanded we are also developing our personalities. It is vital for the all-round development of an individual to feel happy in their chosen career and, more importantly, feel in control of that situation.

Of course it would be a miracle if we all found ourselves in a job that we enjoyed all the time. Most people at some time in their life are unhappy with their work and it is important to strike a balance between when you are just experiencing a touch of the blues or when your employment is seriously starting to affect your health. Individuals often feel discontented after having a break from work such as coming back after a holiday and having to adapt to a change in routine. These blues should quickly disappear once your former routine is established and you look forward once again to the parts of your role that give you most satisfaction. A good rule of thumb to identify whether you are just suffering from a touch of the blues is to put an X in your diary every day you feel unhappy in your job, then, after six weeks have elapsed, look back in your diary and add up the total number of times X appears. If the total number is more than half your total working days, perhaps it is time seriously to consider looking for another job.

Making that key decision to move can often be the hardest part of the whole process of job hunting. Many of us have been in situations where we knew we were unfulfilled and our jobs were making us unhappy, yet we chose to stick our heads in the sand and hope that the situation would improve. If you are the main breadwinner in a family it would be foolhardy to decide to change jobs without putting a lot of thinking and planning into what your next role will be and how you plan to find it. Changing jobs need not be a frightening process; you just need to be mentally prepared for what is ahead.

You may have been propelled into the job-hunting market for reasons outside your control. Perhaps you have just found out that you are facing redundancy or have been dismissed from your job. Both situations can lead to immense stress and worry for you and your family. Where to turn for advice? Will you be able to get another job? What will you do if you don't get a job? All are common questions that can cause you sleepless nights and increase your stress levels to a point where your health can start to become affected.

During the process of career change it is normal to experience a number of often conflicting emotions. These may be compounded by the sense of loss you feel when the decision to change jobs was not made by you. In order to turn your emotions towards positivity it is vital to get in touch with your feelings. Discuss how you feel with someone you trust as this often helps to open up the communication channels that can offer you support and comfort. Keeping your emotions to yourself will result in feelings of isolation and failure, making it harder for you to see the light at the end of the tunnel. As soon as you begin to communicate and identify how you feel, the load will get lighter to bear and you should begin to see the positive aspects of the situation you are in. Perhaps making that career step you've always wanted to do, taking the opportunity to study at college or university? The cycle of emotion will turn in your favour as soon as you accept the situation and take the decision to move on.

Dealing with stress/change

'It's not the situation . . . It's your reaction to the situation.'   Robert Conklin

Dealing with the stress of job hunting is something that we should be prepared for when embarking on this project. It is important to tackle the situation with clear goals in sight and with a plan of attack to help you achieve job-hunting success. You can make it an enjoyable process if you approach it armed with the knowledge and confidence that is vital when presenting yourself to future employers.

Be aware of your current stress levels: are you experiencing any other issues which could affect your ability to be best prepared for job hunting? Why do we often look to change jobs when we have another major upheaval happening in our lives? It is strange but as individuals when one part of our life is changing we seem to want to change everything else at the same time. While this approach is not to be recommended, be aware that if you have no choice and have to change several key factors in your life within a relatively short period of time you will see it through. There are often incidents that happen in our life that we have very little influence over, these incidents help shape our future, good or bad, but we deal with them because we have to.

Recognise that making a job change is stressful, try to identify your level of stress and how you deal with it. The following exercise will help you to build up a picture of your current stress level for each event that has occurred to you over the past 12 months. Allocate the number of points that apply to you from column A to column B.

EVENTS	A	B
Death of partner	100	
Divorce	73	
Separation from partner	65	
Imprisonment	63	
Death of close family member	63	
Personal injury or illness	53	
Marriage	50	
Redundancy/job change	47	
Marital reconciliation	45	
Retirement	45	
Change in health of family member	44	
Pregnancy	40	
Sex difficulties	39	
Gain of new family member	39	
Business readjustment	39	
Change in financial status	38	

EVENTS	A	B
Change in number of arguments with partner	35	
Major mortgage	32	
Foreclosure of mortgage or loan	30	
Change in responsibilities at work	29	
Son or daughter leaving home	29	
Trouble with in-laws	29	
Outstanding personal achievement	28	
Partner begins or stops work	26	
Children begin or end school	26	
Change in living conditions	25	
Revision of personal habits	24	
Trouble with boss	23	
Change in work hours or conditions	20	
Change in residence	20	
Change in schools	20	
Change in recreation	19	
Change in church activities	19	
Change in social activities	18	
Minor mortgage or loan	17	
Changes in sleeping habits	16	
Change in number of family reunions	15	
Change in eating habits	15	
Holidays	13	
Christmas	12	
Minor violations of the law	11	
Sum total in column B		

It is important to recognise the changes that can affect your health. Your scoring will give an indication of the level of stress you are currently experiencing and help you to be aware of it.

YOUR SCORE	WHAT IT MEANS
150–199	When these life change units total 150–199 in any 12-month period, this indicates a mild life crisis and the medical histories of people in this bracket have shown that 37% had an appreciable deterioration in health
200–299	A total of 200–299 has proved to indicate a moderate life crisis and in this group 51% of those studied had changes for the worse in their health
Over 300	Over 300 indicates a major life crisis, and in this group 79% fell ill within the following year
	If you are one of those whose score is regularly bordering the 300 mark, remember that 21% did not become ill. If you have often revelled in change, you will be among the 21% who will be all right. Your working life is currently undergoing a great deal of change. It is essential that you take extra care to look after your health

(*Source:* Holmes and Rahe, *Social Readjustment Rating Scale*)

I included the Holmes and Rahe social readjustment rating scale after a good deal of thought on how it would affect the reader. Some individuals may be concerned after compiling their data and realise that their stress levels are much higher than they had thought. It is better to confront a problem now than leave it until you have less control over the situation. Perhaps take up a sport to get rid of those pent up frustrations, take up yoga, join a club on a subject you have an interest in – in other words find some way of relieving your stress to manageable levels.

Most people thrive on having some level of stress to give themselves challenges and goals to strive for; top-class athletes, for example, continually push themselves to limits outside normal endurance levels. The important factor is to be aware of your stress levels, know why you are enduring them and have them under control.

So you have come to a decision, you definitely want to look for a new job; you understand your stress levels – so let's look at how to identify your goals and aspirations.

Goals and aspirations

'Without goals, and plans to reach them, you are like a ship that has set sail with no destination.'

Fitzhugh Dodson

Sometimes we allow ourselves to become stuck in a rut, almost incapable of doing anything to change our life for the better. Perhaps your job or personal life is getting you down and you feel the need to inject a bit of a zest into the situation. Understanding yourself and identifying your goals and aspirations is the beginning of the process to initiate change. Unfortunately, many of us wander through life without a clear path, we don't know where we want to go or how we will get there. Most of us could look back on our lives and realise that we seem to have got there by accident. We didn't plan; we just seem to have ended up here.

I recently read about a survey carried out in 1953 at Yale University where, among other things, graduates were asked if they had goals for the years ahead. Only 10% replied that they had thought about their goals and only 4% had said that they had written down these goals. Twenty years later the university contacted these students to compile data on what they had achieved since leaving in 1953. The staggering result of the compiled data showed that the 4% who had written down their goals 20 years earlier had achieved more success, both financially and personally, than the other 96% combined!

What is clear from these data is that letting our life happen *by accident* is not the way to achieve the things you want. When we start to take control of our life things will start to happen to move it in the direction you want it to go. It is not sufficient to imagine where you want to be in five years' time and expect it magically to materialise.

The human brain is a complex organ and even now with great advances in medicine we still have a very limited understanding of how it actually works. When you process ideas, for example where you would like to be in five years' time, it will stay in your conscious mind for as long as that idea is deemed to be most important. As soon as something else comes along that is considered more important this great idea is often relegated to the subconscious mind and may even disappear without trace. A good way to make goals and aspirations a reality is to write them down since if you don't record them they will be stored in that backoffice filing cabinet in your brain. By writing down our goals we are consciously reminding ourselves that they are important and that we want to have an awareness of them in the decisions we make in our lives.

Many people believe life is mapped out for us. Perhaps this is the case; however, decisions that you make today will affect where you will be in the future. We can all look back in our life and see when circumstances occurred to change it for the better; if you hadn't made a certain decision then something that is happening in your life today would not have occurred. It could be something as simple as spotting a job advertisement in the newspaper to getting the job and meeting your partner at your new workplace. By writing down your goals you are effectively making a commitment to yourself. Until you commit to something, you have not placed the idea firmly in your conscious mind; by committing you are telling your brain that you are determined that this goal will be achieved. It is not important when making the commitment that you plan exactly how you are going to get there. Leave that aside for the time being. What is important is that you have made a commitment to yourself to achieve something.

Let's say you have decided that you want to change jobs and want to make that one of your committed goals, you may also want to earn £30k a year as well as drive a VW Golf gti. What is important is that you don't have to figure out what job would entail all three goals; you simply have to write down what you want to achieve, display it in a prominent position at home and *make that your commitment*.

I often say to friends that if only it were as easy to believe all the good things about us as it is all the bad things. Our culture has made it easy for us to take a pessimistic view of things that happen around us. How many times have you heard yourself say, 'I can't do that because . . .' before you've even considered whether you *could* do it?

Returning to the subject of athletes, we discussed earlier how they push their stress levels much further than you or I could probably do, because they have a goal that they want to achieve and will push and push until they achieve it. Let's look at boxing – how many boxers have you heard, interviewed prior to the big fight, stating that they didn't think they would win? Not one, I bet! They thrive on self-confidence and belief, every time they step into that ring that are under no doubt that they *will* win. Sometimes they don't win; they often get beaten in front of an audience and on live TV. Does it make them go away and never fight again? No. Before you know it they are back on our TV screens, being interviewed in newspapers, screaming for a rematch. They are supreme masters of self-confidence and will not allow themselves to wallow in self-pity and let the disappointment of losing affect their ability to fight again.

We cover dealing with disappointment later on in the book, but take a moment just now to consider how many opportunities you have passed by because you didn't want to take the chance, didn't want to fail or didn't want to be disappointed.

When approaching your job hunting you must take on all the necessary skills to ensure that you have the edge over your competitors. This means preparing yourself mentally, daring to step outside your comfort zone and approaching the task with vigour and determination.

Well, what are you waiting for? Let's get started.

Analysing your needs and wants

'The difference between the impossible and the possible lies in a person's determination.'

Tommy Lasorda

Why are you looking for a new job? This is the key question to ask yourself. You will be asked this at every interview you attend so let's get it out of the way.

When you decided to buy this book, you were probably looking for a little inspiration to kickstart your job hunting. Perhaps you haven't looked for a while and wanted to freshen up on your skills, you've just been told you are losing your job, perhaps you've had a bad day and decided enough is enough. Whatever your reason for looking, it is important to clarify your thought processes in a manner that you can convey to a future employer.

Interviewers love to talk about your reasons for leaving a role as it gives them clues to your personality and how you view other people. It is a truly open question through the answer to which you will be expected to elaborate on the decision-making process that led you into the job market.

So what *are* your reasons? The easiest place to start is to list your jobs in chronological order and to start to write down next to each one the things you liked about that role and the things that you didn't like. Be honest with yourself, no one else will see this document unless you choose to share it. It is for your eyes only. This information will help you later when you start to compile your CV, so let's include as much detail as you can remember.

I have taken a case study of two individuals who have decided to change roles. These examples should help guide you in the right direction. Joanne is currently working as an administrator in a solicitors' office; she has been employed there for just over two years and wants to identify her next career move. John is currently an engineer in a manufacturing company; he has been employed there for six years and wants to identify if he is just suffering from a touch of the blues or whether it is time to move on.

Joanne's job history, likes and dislikes

Job dates	Job details	Job likes	Job dislikes
Nov 99–present	Administrator – Lee & Brown Solicitors	1 Audio typing 2 Answering the telephone 3 Dealing with correspondence 4 City centre location	1 Don't get on with my boss 2 Low paid 3 Fed up with working in a solicitors' office
Jun 97–Nov 99	Junior administrator – Pecan packaging	1 Working in an office 2 Getting experience and training 3 Answering the telephone 4 Socialising with workmates	1 Low paid 2 No promotion prospects 3 Don't get on with my boss

John's job history, likes and dislikes

Job dates	Job details	Job likes	Job dislikes
Feb 96–present	Engineer – Browns Engineering	1 Well paid 2 Enjoy a laugh with my workmates 3 Finish at 12 noon on a Friday 4 Good holidays	1 Don't get any job satisfaction 2 No training courses available 3 Don't get treated well by management

Job dates	Job details	Job likes	Job dislikes
			4 Difficult to get to workplace by public transport
Jul 92–Feb 96	Apprentice engineer – Mattock Engineering	**1** Put through my apprenticeship **3** Enjoyed earning wages for the first time **4** Good company to work for	**1** Job role changed and I didn't enjoy the work

Now have a look at your likes and dislikes and try to see them through someone else's eyes – what would they see?

By reading into your reasons for leaving previous jobs, you should be able to start building up a picture of your personality and how others see you. Your personality traits, like it or not, are here to stay. We can moderate certain aspects of our behaviour to suit a job role; however, the bulk of your personality cannot be changed to suit specific jobs. But don't panic, all is not lost! If you are aware of your personality traits you can make it easier to find the job or career that really suits you. All too often we ignore what we really like or dislike and find ourselves in a job that does not suit us, which can very quickly lead to unhappiness.

Think back to previous jobs you have had, how many were you sad to leave? If you can say on balance that you were sad to leave a role, then there were major parts of that job and culture that suited your personality type. For those of us who have been unfortunate enough to start a new job and very quickly realise that we are not enjoying it (usually evident within the first three months), this can be very disheartening. Not only have you caused disruption in your life by recently changing roles but you have to consider doing it all again. On reflection, you may now be able to look back and identify why that job was not right for you and, with any luck, avoid making the same mistake in the future.

By learning to identify your likes and dislikes clearly, you can avoid the trap of job hopping. Job hoppers tend to move jobs frequently, feel unfulfilled and have no clear reasoning behind their frequent job changes. Employers tend to be wary of this type of individual; if they were offered a job would they stay long enough for the company to get the benefit of their experience? If you recognise yourself from this description you need to analyse your reasons for leaving roles and make sure that your next step will be the one that is right for you.

By looking at the examples on pages 11–12, can you see why Joanne and John may have made decisions to change jobs?

When Joanne analysed her likes and dislikes she discovered:

■ **She changed her last two jobs because she didn't like the boss**

Her reasoning was that both her previous bosses had been very strict and constantly picked on her work

Could it perhaps be that Joanne is overly sensitive and takes offence easily? Is Joanne difficult to work with? Does Joanne rebel against supervision?

■ **She changed her last two jobs because they were underpaid**

Her reasoning was that she was being paid less than jobs advertised in the local newspaper for the same type of work

Perhaps Joanne was unlucky enough to have two jobs one after the other that did not pay well; however, did she consider what these other roles entailed? Was she suitably qualified for them? Did she have a pay review date? Did she tell her boss she was unhappy with the salary prior to resigning?

■ **Joanne enjoyed audio typing, answering the telephone and being in a city centre location**

She enjoyed the day-to-day tasks of her role, which involved dealing with the public over the telephone, typing reports and being close to the city centre where she could meet friends after work

Joanne enjoyed the skill aspects of her job as an administrator and the city centre location. When Joanne was looking for another job she realised she would make sure that she tried to find another role that involved the day-to-day tasks she enjoyed, while making sure that she was centrally located.

When Joanne analysed her previous job history, likes and dislikes she found that overall she had enjoyed the roles. Her personality had not mixed well with her supervisors and she decided to take a closer look at herself for reasons why they had not got on. She was eager to earn as much money as possible to support her thriving social life, but agreed that perhaps her expectations needed to be more realistic. She agreed that she would attempt to communicate with her supervisor more effectively to ensure a more harmonious work environment.

When John analysed his likes and dislikes he discovered:

■ **He didn't get job satisfaction from his previous two roles**

His reasoning was that he had learnt all there was to learn and felt that the job no longer offered any challenges

John has been in his most recent role for six years and is perhaps ready for a change. He may be the type of personality who requires a challenge in his workplace and when that is taken away he becomes bored. Perhaps he could look for other roles within his current company where he could use his experience to benefit the company and increase his own satisfaction by learning another role.

■ **He finds it difficult to travel by public transport to his place of work**

John's place of work was in an out-of-the-way industrial estate that required him to catch a bus and train every day. It took him over one hour to complete a six-mile journey

John has managed, despite the travelling difficulties, to commute to his place of work for over six years. Perhaps the strain of commuting is being compounded by his lack of interest at the workplace.

■ **He is well paid and enjoys a good relationship with his colleagues**

John is happy with his pay at the end of every month and has a good working relationship with his colleagues, despite feeling badly treated by management

John has been happy with his pay in his previous two jobs and is not money oriented. He has a good working relationship with his colleagues and enjoys the social aspects of his job. He feels that the management at his place of work do not treat the workers well but needs to reflect if it directly affects him and his conditions. If this is the case, does he have a union he could approach? Is management aware of the feelings of the workers? Could he discuss his feelings at his next appraisal?

John may be experiencing a touch of the blues. He is not money oriented, as he has been happy throughout his career with the money he has earned. He seems to enjoy the engineering environment and perhaps needs to find his own form of transport to enable him to cast his net wider in seeking a job that will give him more satisfaction than his current role. He would benefit by discussing his feelings with a supervisor he trusts in order to identify whether there is a place for him in his current company that can fulfil his needs.

Hopefully, you will now have a good idea of why you made decisions in the past to change jobs. If you are having trouble analysing your reasons, ask a friend or family member to help – they are usually the ones you talk to when things are going well or badly, so it's likely they'll be able to give you some pointers.

We have looked at answering that all-important question of 'Why are you looking?' Now we need to find out what your needs and wants as an individual are, in order to ensure you are successful in getting the job that is right for you. In Joanne's and John's case they wanted to leave their current role and had left previous roles for completely different reasons, but those reasons were important enough to them as individuals to initiate a job change.

In the UK today there is a very transient workforce, gone are the days when the male breadwinner worked seven days a week to feed his family while his wife was the homemaker. These days it is far more likely that both parents work to earn a decent standard of living, plus there are many single parents struggling to earn enough money to survive. Everyone has his or her own motivation for going out to work; most of us work because we have to, not because we enjoy it necessarily. If we do enjoy it while we are there, this is very much a bonus.

Throughout this book my aim is to provide you with the tools you need to find the job that satisfies your needs as an individual and fulfils your wishlist. Many of us never stop to think about satisfying our own needs, but these must be taken into account with all those other key factors that make up your perfect job. The perfect job does exist; it is just a matter of identifying it.

During my years in the recruitment sector I identified the top ten reasons why individuals enter the job market. Can you identify with any of these?

1 I want to earn more money.

2 I find my current job does not satisfy my needs.

3 I want to gain more experience and my current company cannot provide it.

4 I want to work closer to home.

5 I am ready for a promotion and there are no opportunities at my current company.

6 I want to work for a bigger/smaller organisation.

7 I don't get on with my boss.

8 I want to work fewer/more hours.

9 I want to change my career completely.

10 I am not appreciated at my current company.

In order to identify your own personal needs/wants write down on a piece of paper what you want to achieve on a personal level from your next job move. Next, identify from your needs/wants the three points that are the most important to you and your circumstances. These points will make up your wishlist, so no matter what other benefits a job may have it must contain these three items.

The reason why it is important to make up your wishlist is that it is all too easy when you start out on the job hunt to forget *why* you started it in the first place. We get swept along on the tide of excitement and before we know it we are back where we started – in a job that is not suited! By sticking to your wishlist you take control of your career and move it in the direction you want to go. Of course, circumstances do change so if you feel that a more important factor has emerged, change your wishlist to cope with it. But (and this is very important) ensure that you put the same amount of thought and understanding into the compilation every time.

We will go through the whole interview process in more detail in a later chapter, but for now try to put yourself in the interviewers' shoes for a moment. They are very keen to delve into your reasons for leaving previous roles so they don't make a mistake in hiring you and you don't make a mistake in going to work there. The whole purpose of an interview from the employers' perspective is to find an individual who:

- has the skills to do the job
- will be able to use those skills to do the job
- has the personality that will fit into the company.

In other words: Can you do the job? Will you do the job? Will you fit in?

By looking at your reasons for leaving you should be able to highlight any shortcomings you may need to address and match your likes and dislikes against any interesting jobs you see. You should then aim to target your job-hunting skills towards the areas that suit your personality and career aspirations.

In interview situations it is important to be honest about why you left previous jobs, it shows a certain maturity to be able to look back at previous roles and perhaps see where you would have acted differently if you had the opportunity again. As long as you can show a clear and logical thinking path behind each job move your interviewer should be satisfied and move on to other aspects of your career.

Which direction – same job/different company or same company/different job?

'Even if you're on the right track, you'll get run over if you just sit there.'   **Will Rogers**

By now you should be well on your way to identifying what is important to you in terms of your goals and aspirations as well as your needs and wants. Every individual is different and by taking the time out to reflect on your desires you should be much better equipped to plan your next move.

So do you look for a completely different job outside your present organisation or do you attempt to find another role with your current employer? Never an easy question to answer and you are the only one who can do so after weighing up the pros and cons of your current situation.

If you are happy with your present organisation's culture but are simply in need of a change, is there anyone you can identify who may be able to help you investigate current opportunities? Recruitment in the UK costs businesses billions of pounds every year and most forward-thinking organisations will do everything they can to keep their employees. In my experience, many organisations publish internal vacancy listings or promote contact with an HR representative to encourage their workers to seek opportunities with them rather than lose their expertise to another organisation.

If you are not happy with your present organisation or can see no way of investigating internal vacancies discreetly then perhaps it is time to make the decision to look for opportunities elsewhere.

The main factor to consider here is to ensure that you have weighed up the advantages and disadvantages of both avenues before arriving at your decision. A committed job hunter will succeed much more quickly and effectively than someone who sits on the fence faced by indecision and 'what ifs'. Investigate both areas and you can then move forward with the knowledge that you are completely committed to the tasks ahead.

The job-hunting cycle

'Great things are not done by impulse, but by a series of small things brought together.'

Vincent van Gogh

When setting out on the journey of job hunting I find it helps to compare it to an imaginary wheel I call the job-hunting cycle, which should give you a good visual impression of where your levels of influence lie. By identifying where you can make a difference you can make the whole process a much easier and enjoyable experience.

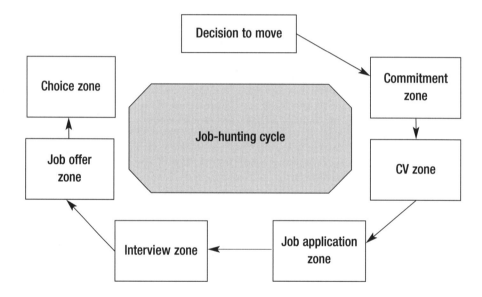

You have control over a number of the sections outlined in the cycle, while the employer controls the remainder. Can you identify your control zones?

The first part of the job-hunting cycle has already begun – *the decision to move.*

If you made the decision to look for employment you will have controlled this sector. If the decision was taken for you, for example if you were made redundant or dismissed from your position, the employer will have controlled this sector.

The second stage of the job-hunting cycle is the *commitment zone*. This zone is completely under your control. Remember back to our discussion of top-class athletes and their inner stress level control and extremely high standards of commitment to their chosen profession? Imagine how much these individuals would achieve if they displayed a lacklustre attitude. How successful would an athlete be who survived on a diet of junk food and was regularly seen out nightclubbing before a big event? Just like athletes in pursuit of their dream of being the best, you have the power to take control of your job hunting by displaying absolute commitment to the journey ahead.

The third stage of the job-hunting cycle is the *CV zone*. The production of a great CV rests completely in your hands. The amount of effort you commit to this zone will have a direct influence on how far you proceed around the job-hunting cycle.

The fourth stage of the job-hunting cycle is the *job application zone*. Only you can apply for jobs, so you have complete control over this sector.

The fifth stage of the job-hunting cycle is the *interview zone*. You have entered the job market, displayed your commitment, produced a knockout CV and applied for the job you want. The employer now holds the control at this stage: Whether to call you forward for interview? When to see you? What time to see you? Where to meet? The employer normally has no control whatsoever in the four stages leading up to this sector, yet, despite their almost complete control over this zone you still have an influencing factor card to play – your performance at interview.

The sixth stage of the job-hunting cycle is the *job offer zone*. Your interview performance will be your trump card over every other candidate who enters the job offer zone. The employer's ultimate decision on who to offer the job to will be based on your performance at interview. Both you and the employer share control over this sector with each of you having a part to play in the outcome of the process.

The final stage of the job-hunting cycle is the *choice zone*. Your ability successfully to master control over the previous zones has given you the ultimate control – choice.

Getting started

'Talk doesn't cook rice.'   **Chinese proverb**

We have covered a lot of the thinking behind changing jobs in this section. Some of it may have made painful reading for you, self-analysing is never an easy process as you may find out some things you don't like; by being honest about your aspirations and personality you can change the course of your life and take control of your career.

It is much better to be shown the road to follow than have to stumble along it alone; none of us has been to the school of life that teaches you how to get that perfect job. Until now you have probably survived on the pieces of advice you may have received from family and friends, but perhaps never really felt like you had the complete picture.

In addition to the job-hunting cycle where each zone has its level of influence, imagine this whole process is like setting out on a 110m-hurdle race. As you take off from the starting blocks you have a number of hurdles to jump over before you finally get to the finishing line. You may not be interested in completing it in the fastest possible time, but what is important is that you have the stamina and ability to make it to the finishing line. Each stage of the job-hunting process is comparable to jumping over a hurdle; it is important to take each stage as it comes and concentrate on completing it before attempting to jump the next hurdle.

This book aims to provide you with a complete view of every stage of the process, helping you to understand for the first time the true secrets of getting ahead in the job market.

Now is the time to feel inspired – you are setting out on a new journey armed with information about yourself.

2 Preparing and writing your CV

'We are continually faced by great opportunities brilliantly disguised as insoluble problems.'

Lee Iacocca

What is a CV?

The abbreviation CV is adopted from the Latin: *curriculum* meaning running, a contest in running, race, course of action, and *vitae* meaning life, career, livelihood, mode of life.

It may be a number of years since you have looked for a new job, perhaps when you last applied CVs weren't around or were completely different to how you have been advised they look today. Your CV is a representation of the real you and is your opportunity directly to communicate with an employer about your skills, experiences and achievements. It is important that you put a great deal of thought into the preparation of your CV in order to ensure that you produce a document which sells your qualities and makes the employer want to see you.

Imagine your CV as the first stage of your plan to securing the job you want. It may be the only opportunity you get to represent yourself to an employer, so it has to be right every time. You should approach the whole job-hunting process in stages, where each stage allows you to proceed to the next, remembering the importance of achieving one before you set your sights on the next:

- Good applications – get you interviews.
- Good interviews – get you jobs.
- Good job offers – give you choices.

Producing a knockout CV is one of the few stages of the job-hunting process in which you have absolute control.

While I was researching my material for this book I came across an interesting fact that you may not be aware of. If you read a book or document that has been written by an American author or surf the internet and come across an American-oriented site, the contents and meaning of a CV in the UK are different from in the USA. What we know as a CV in the UK would be known as a resumé in the USA; the term CV is only applicable to academic and scientific positions and takes on a very different format from what we identify as a CV. So beware if you take advice from any of these sites or books – they may not be relevant to the UK marketplace.

You may decide to take the easy course of action and have someone else prepare your CV for you. There are a number of sites on the internet and many newspaper advertisements offering to compile and type your CV for you. Apart from the obvious cost of these services, what you need to consider very seriously is whether they can represent you adequately on paper, in order to get you the interview you want. Unless you put the document together yourself and use them merely as a typing service, I would strongly recommend that you compile your own CV. Creating your own CV and the thought process that goes behind it will give you ownership over the document and instil the sense of confidence you will need in interview situations.

CV facts – true or false?

As we previously discussed, your CV is a representation of you on paper, written with the aim of securing an interview. In my experience there are some common misconceptions about CVs:

- My CV should contain all my previous jobs, together with details of my skills and experience.
- The more information I include on my CV the better.
- My CV will be read with interest by every employer who receives it.
- My CV will get me the job I want.
- My CV would be prepared better by a professional service.
- My CV content is more important than its appearance.
- My CV will be more effective if I tell a few white lies.
- My CV should be at least three pages long.
- My CV should include a recent photograph.
- My CV should be in my own handwriting.

Let's take each one of these statements and discuss them in more detail.

My CV should contain all my previous jobs, together with details of my skills and experience

Your CV is your passport to an interview; it should contain relevant details that are applicable to that job. Be wary of listing every job you have ever done with full details of your skills and experience in each. You may be applying for a role that is in no way connected to one you had ten years ago. The employer is looking to identify your key skills in order to decide whether to invite you forward for interview. Previously, when we talked about what an employer is looking for when recruiting staff, we highlighted that one of the key indicator's is whether you *can do* the job. It is vital to ensure that the employer can see straightaway that you have the necessary skills and experience and does not get bogged down with irrelevant information. List jobs that are unconnected to the position you are applying for by simply stating the dates of employment, job title, position and in no more than two sentences condense your skills within this role. I should point out that it is important to include these jobs so that the employer can follow your career path. Unexplained gaps could indicate that you are trying to hide something, for example a spell spent 'at Her Majesty's Pleasure'!

The more information I include on my CV the better

Too much information is as damaging as too little information and may give the indication that you are padding out a weak application. Make the CV easy to read and supply the reader with the information that is relevant to the position. Include any detail that directly shows that you have the experience and skills to do the job. Do not be misguided and include every training course and hobby you have ever undertaken during your career. Remember: be relevant and stand out from the crowd.

My CV will be read with interest by every employer who receives it

Not true. If advertising directly for staff, employers may receive hundreds if not thousands of CVs in response. They will scan the CVs looking for specific skills and knowledge that indicate that the individual *can do* the job. You may only get this opportunity once, so it is important to grab the employer's attention within the first few seconds of reading.

My CV will get me the job I want

Not true. The primary reason for producing a CV is to get you the interview; a good CV will not get you the job. Be sure to separate in your mind the difference between getting the interview and getting the job. Many people approach the whole job-hunting process from completely the wrong direction and become frustrated when they are not invited forward for interviews, all too often focusing on getting the job without putting adequate care and attention into the production of their CVs.

My CV would be prepared better by a professional service

Not true. Who knows you best of all? You! There are many CV-writing services advertising on the internet and in newspapers. Many of these are simply secretarial facilities that will compile your CV into a predetermined format that may be totally unsuitable for your purpose. If you are unable to have your CV typed locally and have no choice but to use one of these organisations, be sure to handwrite and compile your own CV and state that you require it to be produced in the format you request.

My CV content is more important than its appearance

Not true. Previously we talked about the fact that a potential employer would likely allocate only a couple of seconds when scanning your CV for relevant information. Your CV is a representation of you, what would it tell the employer if it arrived as a badly photocopied sheet with dirty marks on it? No matter how well your CV is written the presentation of that document is equally important to convey the right impression of you as an individual. You may have read that you should send your CV on brightly coloured paper or add some graphics to make it stand out from the crowd. That may be the case and the employer would certainly notice it, but does this convey the impression you want to create? Imagine a city banker sending his CV to a prospective employer on bright pink paper. Would the employer see him as a professional, capable of representing his company at high-powered meetings? More likely he would not be taken seriously; he may have stood out but he has not created the impression he would have desired. From my experience I would recommend that all CVs be produced on good quality white paper, irrespective of the role you are applying for. At the point of sending your CV to an employer you have no real indication of what their personality is like, therefore it would be advisable to err on the side of caution and send your CV on white paper. There are of course exceptions to this rule, for example if you would be required as part of the role to be creative and want to show the employer what you can do. Use your common sense and apply whichever you feel is relevant to the position you are applying for.

My CV will be more effective if I tell a few white lies

Not true. People may tell you that it is OK, it will make you stand out from the crowd, but don't be fooled. Little white lies have been known to cost individuals their jobs in the past, often when it was completely unnecessary to have told the white lie in the first place. The primary objective of any interview situation is that the interviewer gains as full a picture of you as possible and that means probing your background, skills and experiences to find out what really makes you tick. You may have been tempted to exaggerate your experience in order to get to the interview stage and feel that you can brush over it when there. There has been many a case where an individual has been made to feel very uncomfortable during an interview when it becomes apparent to the interviewer that, for example, their experience is not quite as extensive as it was made out to be on their CV. Not only would you in all likelihood blow any chances of getting the job, but would have wasted both your and the interviewer's time. Do not become confused with pointing out your key skills and achievements on your CV; they are an important part of the document and as such will bolster your chances of being invited for interview. What is important is to be able to quantify any claims you make, for example: 'I achieved a 120% growth in turnover within 12 months of joining Smith's Sales & Co.'

Your interviewer would expect to ask you about how you managed to achieve this, what skills you brought into play, who else was involved in the achievement etc. Ensure that you can back up what you put on your CV with fact.

My CV should be at least three pages long

Your CV is not about length but the quality of the information it contains. In order to grab the employer's attention when scanning CVs it is vital to grab their attention in the first page. Imagine your CV made it into the *yes* pile of CVs that had arrived in the post that morning. The employer will likely have a second look at these CVs in order to whittle down the numbers to include individuals they definitely want to see. You have caught their eye at the initial phase and do not want to bore them with pages and pages of detail that they may consider irrelevant. It is also equally important that if your CV is too short it may fail to sell your qualities adequately. Remember too much detail is as damaging as too little. I would recommend that you attempt to produce a CV that is around two or three pages in length.

My CV should include a recent photograph

Very much an American idea that has made its way to our shores over the past few years. There is no doubt that a picture will make you stick in the mind of the employer and as such you are more likely to be remembered. I would recommend against including a photograph for one simple reason – the employer may discriminate against you on the grounds of how you look.

My CV should be in my own handwriting

On the few occasions I have received handwritten CVs instead of the normal typed versions my immediate reaction has been to put them to one side. Handwritten CVs can damage your chances of obtaining an interview, as they do not afford the same professional feel of typewritten versions. You may think that your handwriting is legible and easy to follow but if the employer has difficulty in reading your writing you have almost certainly blown your chances of gaining an interview. I would strongly recommend finding some way of typing your CV for presentation to an employer. The only occasions when handwritten versions are deemed acceptable is when you are specifically asked to apply in your own handwriting or when completing an application form.

Identifying your skills and achievements

'Attitude determines altitude.'   Anon

You should by this stage have started to build up a picture in your mind of the skills and achievements you have identified from previous jobs and situations. The easy part would be to simply write them down and get on with it! But it's never that easy is it?

Remember how your brain works, it is like a massive computer continually storing information from everything that goes on around it. It is now time to activate that computer and retrieve information from your memory banks, enabling you to identify what your skills and achievements are. Your skills and achievements can also come from outside the workplace; you could, for example, display leadership and teamwork qualities as the manager of a local football club or sailing team. You may be thinking about moving up to a supervisory position; even though you may not have these skills and experience in the workplace you may be able to demonstrate them in another environment.

To get started the first thing you need to do is get a blank piece of paper and write down your last job title at the top of the page, together with the company you work for and the dates of employment. As job titles can mean different things to different people, imagine you were describing on paper what that job entailed to your best friend (who knows nothing about your line of work). Let's say, for example, you imagine yourself walking in to work; what is your first duty once you get there? As you see yourself going through the working day, jot down all these tasks on your piece of paper. Don't worry about making logical sense of it at the moment; what is important is to write down every task you were involved in. Next, do exactly the same process for any tasks you would carry out on a weekly and monthly basis. Also, include a separate piece of paper for any activities you are involved in outside the workplace. These key pieces of information will help you to identify the key skills and knowledge base that make up the bulk of the CV compilation process. This exercise will help to supply you with an abundance of information, all about you and, more importantly, help you to identify where your aspirations and potential lie.

Sally is currently working at Brown's Greeting Cards Ltd as a secretary. She has compiled her working routines into worksheets to help her identify her skills.

Sally's daily/ weekly/monthly worksheets

Job title: Secretary

Company: Brown's Greeting Cards Ltd

Dates: Jan 97–present

Daily tasks

1   Open up the office
2   Check for messages on the answering machine
3   Open morning post and stamp with date of receipt

4   Allocate morning post to business managers

5   Answer the telephone and deal with customer queries

6   Type 20-page report for sales development manager using MS Word

7   Attend 10am meeting and take minutes

8   Type up minutes of meeting

9   Telephone various caterers to obtain quotes for client lunch next week

10 Type up quotes and pass to sales development manager for perusal

11 Deal with members of the public visiting the showroom

12 File items of mail in the filing cabinet

13 Produce sales projections document for the sales director using MS Excel

Weekly tasks

1   Balance petty cash and produce report for managing director using
    MS Excel spreadsheet

2   Produce mailshot for sales director using MS Word and Excel

3   Organise collection of mailshot by distribution company

4   Organise stationery requirements and place order using Lotus Notes email

Monthly tasks

1   Collect sales figures from company representatives by telephone

2   Produce monthly sales figures and performance charts for managing director using MS Excel
    and Word documents.

3   Distribute 60 copies of monthly sales figures document internally and externally

Hobbies and interests

1   Leader of Brownie pack two evenings a week – have been involved in running Brownie pack
    for five years

2   Have a computer at home and often use the internet and MS Outlook email to speak to
    friends around the country

Sally has been employed at Browns Greeting Cards Ltd for four years and has decided that she wants to progress up the career ladder, possibly to a PA position. On looking through her task sheets she has identified the following skills that she could include in her CV:

- good knowledge of MS Word
- experience in producing spreadsheets and reports on MS Excel
- good typing skills
- experience in taking minutes
- key holder
- experience in coordinating lunchtime conferences
- experience in dealing with members of the public face to face and over the telephone
- responsibility for the smooth running of the office including filing and distribution of mail items both within the company and to external customers
- responsibility for the £50 petty cash float and direct accountability to the MD
- leadership qualities and commitment by running a Brownie pack for five years
- confidence in the use of internet and corresponding by email using Lotus Notes and MS Outlook.

Already Sally feels more confident about what information she can include in her CV by simply listing her tasks at home and work.

Sally is an example of a secretarial candidate and while her job role may have little in common with the job you currently do, take her worksheets as an example of how simple it can be to compile the key information you will need when starting to write your CV.

Next we want to take a look at your achievements, facts that you should include on your CV to make the employer want to invite you for interview. Some of us are very reluctant to include achievements, scared of being labelled 'big headed' or 'arrogant', but achievements are a surefire way to propel you into the interview stage so don't be hesitant about blowing your own trumpet. If you want the interview – ask for it!

We have previously discussed the importance of making your CV stand out to an employer, when they are likely to have a number of applications for their vacancy. The employer may be able to see from your skills that you *can do* the job; their objective is to find out if you *will do* it. This is usually explored in more detail during the interview process, but by highlighting your achievements on your CV you are providing the employer with quantifiable proof, increasing your chances of being invited for interview. We have all come across individuals in our work and personal lives who are perfectly capable of doing a task – on paper they would seem to have all the key indicators that would indicate success. However, when it comes down to the actual daily tasks of the role, they may be careless, lacklustre and well below the level you would expect. A new employer does not want to inherit an individual who may turn out to be a liability to their company. Recruitment is an expensive process that costs employers billions of pounds every year.

In order to give you an understanding of the processes involved in recruitment, let's look at the tasks an employer would have to follow in order to recruit a member of staff:

- Identify the need for the vacancy.
- Decide on method of advertising.
- Produce a job description and person specification.
- Produce an advertisement to sell the vacancy to potential candidates.
- Allocate a sum of money for the advertising costs.
- Allocate time to look through CVs received.
- Decide who to invite for first interviews.
- Allocate time to interview candidates.
- Reply to unsuccessful candidates.
- Decide who to invite for second interviews.
- Allocate time to interview candidates.
- Reply to unsuccessful candidates.
- Make offer to successful candidate.
- Arrange for training (including health and safety) when new employee commences work.
- Monitor and provide ongoing training for new employee (first three months of employment).

The employer recruitment tasklist is not intended to scare you! Having an awareness of the procedures an employer has to follow during the hiring process affords you the benefit of understanding how the job-hunting trail starts and ends, for both parties. The more knowledge you have, the more prepared you will be.

The employer wants to find the right person to fill their vacancy and in order to do that he or she knows that they will have to allocate time and effort to achieve it. They should be able to see from your CV that you have both the skills and the knowledge they are looking for, but they cannot check whether you have the ability to perform the role to the standard required. The only indication an employer has to your ability are your past achievements. Your achievements prove that you have the ability to apply your skills and knowledge to the task at hand and should give them some confidence that you *will do* the job.

As before when identifying your skills and knowledge, let's look at the worksheet you compiled that listed your previous jobs and daily tasks. Identifying achievements is the one area where we often become stuck, because we often perform our jobs without identifying when we made a difference. Look at your worksheets again to try to answer the following questions to get those memory banks working to retrieve stored information.

Remember back to a time when you were praised for something you had done at work. What did you do? How did it benefit your employers?

Do you work to targets? Have you ever overachieved your targets?

Have you ever come up with an idea in work that improved processes and efficiency? Did your employer adopt it? What impact did it make on the company, e.g. in terms of time, cost savings etc.?

Have you ever received any awards or been formally recognised for your work?

Have you ever been promoted? Why?

How have you adapted to changes within your work environment?

Have you produced output above your colleagues' average? By how much?

Do you have an outstanding attendance record? Over what period of time?

As we have previously discussed, your achievements will make you stand out to an employer and it is important to highlight achievements that are relevant when responding to a job advertisement.

Features and benefits

In order to reflect how your achievements will sell your ability to an employer, let's take an example of when you decide to make a purchase. You have made the decision that you want to buy your first car; you have only just passed your driving test and are a little vague about the type of car you want. The key indicator for you is the amount of money you have allocated to the purchase, let's say it is £2,000. The purchase is to enable you to travel 30 miles back and forward to work every day, so you need to be sure that the car is reliable. You make a trip to the local car showroom and the salesperson is eager to show you the cars they have on display. They start by asking you questions about the car you would like in order to identify the key requirements you have. The salesperson then identifies from your answers the type of car you are looking for and mentally matches up the cars he/she has available to show you. The salesperson will identify the features and benefits of each car in order to make the sale, for example:

Feature	This car has a full service history.
Benefit	The car has been regularly serviced which indicates it has been looked after and is reliable.
Feature	This car has ABS brakes.
Benefits	The ABS brakes will control the car without skidding, which enhances its safety aspects.
Feature	This car has power steering.
Benefits	Power steering makes the car easier to manoeuvre.

People buy benefits, not features. By pointing out the benefits the salesperson is highlighting the reasons why you should buy a particular car. The fact that you are a learner driver should make you more conscious of the safety aspects of driving; ABS brakes and power steering will give you added confidence; you have some distance to travel to work every day and need a car that is reliable, so the benefit of a regular service history should give you added confidence. The salesperson has done their well by pointing out the benefits of the car based on what you said you wanted – in other words they have given you a reason to buy.

When compiling your CV bear in mind that you are attempting to give the employer a reason to buy – i.e. to invite you forward for interview. When thinking about your achievements you need to ascertain which are features and which are benefits. The benefits are the key indicators that will make your CV stand out; they make you different from anyone else who may possess the same set of skills as you. Think about any tasks you have undertaken in your role that brought a benefit to your employer by referring back to your answers on the achievements worksheet; for example, increased their revenue, made a working practice less time consuming etc. Your features and benefits could look something like this:

Feature	Sales manager responsible for recruiting and training a team of five sales consultants.
Benefit	Under my direction the team achieved 150% of target in our first year of operation.
Feature	Production operative in a large food processing plant.
Benefit	Regularly exceeded production figures 15% above factory average.
Feature	Customer service operator with a large call centre environment.
Benefit	Part of a team of six which achieved an outstanding recognition award.

Transferable skills

'Sometimes we are limited more by attitude than by opportunities.'   **Anon**

Transferable skills are defined as skills and knowledge that you can transfer from one employer to another. If you have been in your current role for a number of years you may be under the opinion that because your job was so specialised, you couldn't possibly sell these skills on to another employer. This is not always the case and it is likely that you will be surprised when you begin to compile your job data, that in fact many of these skills are transferable.

To show you how easy it is, let's take the example of an individual leaving the Royal Navy after a career in the Submarine Service. We'll call him Colin. Colin has spent 12 years working as a sonar operator, rising to the rank of petty officer. Colin left school without any formal qualifications and is worried that his specialised career path severely limits the types of job he could apply for. Colin decided to complete his daily/weekly and monthly worksheets to identify his skills and achievements. He was pleasantly surprised to find that he had many skills and achievements that would be of benefit to a future employer. Colin identified:

- responsibility for managing a team of six individuals on a rotating shift basis
- accountability for financial accounts and organising functions as the treasurer of the submarine social fund
- ability to both operate and carry out maintenance on a complex computer system
- ability to problem solve
- regularly reporting directly to board level
- promotion twice in his career.

Colin is now confident enough to start compiling his CV because he has identified his transferable skills and achievements.

Whether you are a deep sea diver, have recently left the armed forces or are moving into a completely new arena of work you should be able to identify some key skills that can be cross-transferred to another employer. If you are having trouble, complete the following worksheet to help you to identify what yours could be. All skills are transferable, it is just a matter of identifying what yours are.

Transferable skills worksheet

Communication skills – Who do you regularly communicate with as part of your current/previous job roles? What qualities do these skills require you to possess, e.g. liaison with varying levels of staff?

Negotiation skills – Do you have to negotiate with different people on a regular basis? Explain the importance of where your negotiating skills make a difference to your employer

---

Accountability skills – Do you have staff directly reporting to you? What specific parts of your job roles are you solely accountable for?

Problem-solving skills – Are you called on to solve problems as part of your daily role? Explain how these skills make a difference to your employer

---

Multitasking skills – Are you required to have the knowledge and ability to complete several tasks as part of your daily role?

Presentation skills – Have you ever been required to present information/ideas to a past employer? What level did you present to? What was the outcome of your presentation?

The examples outlined are just a few of the types of skill that could be transferable from one employer to another. Every job is different, but hopefully these will set your mind working in the right direction and allow you to identify your own, unique transferable skills.

Preparing to put it down on paper

'People who say it cannot be done should not interrupt those who are doing it.'

Anon

During the last few sections we have pulled together various pieces of information that will help you to identify your skills and achievements. You may have made demands on your brain to recall details that you had not thought about for a long time, but the important point is that you should now be armed with enough information about yourself to compile a knockout CV.

Before we begin to summarise the information that you want to include in your CV, refer back to the section on analysing your needs and wants (in Chapter 1) where we discussed identifying the reasons why you want to move jobs, as well as attempting to come up with three key factors that you wish your next role to contain. These key factors make up your most important things (MITs) and should be borne in mind for every role you apply for. Remember that staying close to your MITs will help you to focus on your career and personal aspirations as well as keeping you on the right track towards achieving the type of job that will best suit you. Everyone has different reasons for leaving a job, some of which could be personal or career-related. What is important is to identify what they are and stick close to them in your next career move. In the section on analysing your needs and wants we discussed some of the most common reasons people look to change jobs. Can you identify three key factors that you consider vital when considering your next move? For example:

1 city centre location
2 flexible working hours
3 senior administration position.

If your MITs focus around career progression and your aspirations for the future, take a look in your local newspaper at jobs being advertised – have you identified any particular roles that you may be interested in? What sort of skills and knowledge are employers looking for in these particular roles – can you identify any similarities against the skills and achievements you have attained to date?

During the section on identifying your skills and achievements (earlier in this chapter), we looked at the case of Sally who wanted to move up the career ladder from a secretarial position towards a personal assistant role. Sally's worksheets identified that she already possessed most of the skills requested in job advertisements for personal assistant roles. As part of Sally's preparation towards compiling her CV she has already identified what employers are looking for (on paper at least) and highlighted which of these skills would be appropriate for this type of application.

Remember, if you find that you seem not to have the skills necessary for the role you desire, find out what you *do* need to do to bring your skills up to the required level. You may find that you have to gain more experience or a qualification before progressing to that level, perhaps your primary goal would be to seek a role that will act as a steppingstone on to where you want to be.

Your assets to an employer are your skills, knowledge and achievements. Keep reminding yourself of these facts as you begin to compile your CV.

When asking yourself what information you should include on your CV there are only three key areas to consider:

- SKILLS

- ACHIEVEMENTS

- RELEVANCE.

As we previously discussed the employer is interested in finding out whether you *can do* the job. In order to do this they must invite candidates forward for interview who have the necessary skills and knowledge, as well as identifiable achievements that indicate that they *will do* the job. The information that will make your CV stand out from the crowd must include both skills and achievements but also bear relevance to the position you are applying for.

Think back to earlier when we discussed the likelihood of an employer receiving hundreds of CV responses to a job vacancy, how many of these CVs would include only information that is relevant to the position, as well as the necessary skills and achievements? You have the ability to be different by providing the employer with the information they are seeking.

When looking for advice on how your CV should look and what it should contain, almost everyone you speak to will give you a different opinion. There are a wide range of books, magazines and online sites promising to come up with a better CV and give you better advice than any other product in the market. CVs are a matter of personal taste and opinion, as long as you remember the three key words (skills, achievements and relevance) and follow my advice you will be able to produce the type of CV that will virtually guarantee you an interview.

Key CV detail

Imagine your CV is a sales brochure that has just popped through your letterbox. It is designed to catch the eye and highlight the benefits to you as a consumer in buying that product. The intention of a CV is exactly the same – you are attempting to communicate with an employer by highlighting your benefits in order to be invited for interview.

First impressions are as vital in a sales brochure as they are in a CV. What impression would the sales brochure make if it were printed on cheap coloured paper with a spelling mistake on it? The sales brochure company proclaims to consist of master craftsmen, specialists in their field; it is likely you would disagree based on a sample of their work so far. Your CV, like the sales brochure, is a representation of you on paper; it must give the reader an excellent first impression of you as an individual.

Before we move on to the subject of CV styles and layouts, it would be wise to consider what key information your CV should contain in addition to your skills and achievements. By building up a mental picture of your CV you can identify the key parts that will make you stand out to an employer. Let's take a look at the types of information commonly included in a CV and discuss their importance and relevance to you.

Personal information

Personal information is included on your CV to provide the employer with your key details as well as an indication of your personal circumstances. I recommend dividing your personal details section into two distinct areas, primary and secondary. Your primary personal details should be facts that the employer must know when your CV receives its initial ten-second glance on receipt and your secondary personal details contain information that bears some relevance to the position you are applying for and that the employer may be interested in discussing at interview. Primary information should appear on the first page of your CV and secondary information on the final page. It is important not to bog down your CV with irrelevant personal details at the beginning as it will take the employer's eye off the important and relevant facts you want to highlight.

Name

The employer needs to know who you are; your name should be the first detail at the top of your CV. If you think that your name could be used against you in a discriminatory manner refer to the section later on dealing with discrimination.

Address

The employer will need a contact postal address for you and often want to know where you currently reside, usually to take into account how far away from the place of work you live.

Telephone/email contact

The employer may want to make contact with you other than via post, so provide them with the means to do so.

Driving licence details

If the position you are applying for stated that you must hold a specific type of driving licence then include as primary information, if not include as secondary information.

Date of birth

There is no law in the UK governing age discrimination, but some individuals, consciously or not, do practise it and will discriminate against you using your age as a basis. Include as secondary information to allow the employer to read through your skills and achievements before arriving at the information. Don't be tempted to leave the information out as some employers may assume you have something to hide.

Marital status/children

This information will not indicate to the employer how well you can do your job. It is entirely up to you whether you choose to include it or not by reflecting on whether it is relevant to the role you are applying for.

Education details

Unless you are within your first five years of work after school/university, I would suggest that your education details are included as secondary personal information. As you progress in your career your education will become less and less important to an employer and will be overtaken by your skills and achievements. As with employment history if you do include your education details then list them with the most recent first and then work backwards. Beware of using qualification abbreviations that the employer may not understand. The employer will scan your education details for qualifications that they may consider useful to them, so don't be tempted to include everything you have ever done in the hope that one may come in handy! Remember: be relevant to the role you are applying for.

Hobbies and interests

Your hobbies and interests will tell the employer a lot about you, for example are you a team player or do your hobbies indicate solitary pastimes? Include your interests but be sure not to give the impression that your out-of-work activities leave little time for anything else and remember that the interviewer may want to discuss your hobbies in more detail, so don't be tempted to include something that you know little about in the hope of seeming more interesting!

Health

There is no need to include your state of health in a CV since it is assumed that if you apply for a job then your standard of health would not affect your ability to do the job. If you are registered disabled (despite the law, people do still discriminate) I would suggest omitting the information and only bring it to the attention of the employer when arranging your interview, for example when access is required for wheelchair users. Obviously, where the posts you are applying for is specifically detailed for disabled people then include relevant details.

References

I would recommend leaving out any mention of your referees on your CV. When the employer requires these details they will ask for them. The world of references and referees are minefields for both employers and employees due to the legal implications they carry. Most employers these days will only confirm dates of employment and job titles in writing to protect themselves against possible litigation, but will often 'unofficially' be prepared to answer questions about you over the telephone. I would recommend that you contact your referees prior to passing details to your future employer in order to discuss the position with them.

Highlight your areas of skill and achievements that match up against the position you are applying for. Be careful when supplying any reference details prior to being offered the position – imagine if your current employer were contacted while you were still in their employ. Always protect yourself and your current position. Perhaps you could suggest an alternative referee to your current employer if it is imperative that a reference be obtained prior to the job offer stage?

Photographs

As discussed earlier your photograph will certainly make you stand out to an employer. I am not a great fan of photographs as they can be used in a discriminatory manner and in my opinion a passport-sized photograph cannot tell any employer how well you can do your job. If you are asked to send a photograph along with your CV/application form then ask yourself why the employer considers it important at this stage of the process.

Reasons for leaving

Do not include your reasons for leaving previous roles in your CV. The interview process is designed to discuss your previous jobs and your reasons for leaving. You may unintentionally highlight negative information and sabotage any chance you had of being invited for interview.

Salary information

Do not include your current salary information in your CV. If you are asked for this information in a job advertisement, ask yourself why the employer wants to know. In my experience employers who do not advertise salary bands in their advertisements either have no clear idea how much they need to pay to get the person they want or are deliberately attempting to get the best possible fit for the cheapest price! Recruitment agencies differ from employers in that they will act as your agent in matching you against their job vacancies, so it is essential for them to be aware of your current salary and future expectations to conduct negotiations on your behalf and achieve the best possible outcome for all concerned.

Profile/banner heading

Your profile or banner heading is one of the key pieces of information that makes your CV stand out to an employer. It should be no more than two sentences long and is the first key piece of information that an employer will read about you. It instantly affords the employer an opportunity to compare your skills and achievements against your fellow applicants. Your profile is in effect your opportunity to highlight to the employer that you are a good match for the job.

This is the section that most people tend to struggle with, perhaps because it is in effect a 'sales pitch' all about you. In much the same way as a sales brochure with a catchy phrase would hold your attention, your CV should hold the employer's attention and spark a good level of interest, encouraging the employer to read on. Your profile should agree with the rest of your CV, for example if you state in your profile that you are a highly experienced supervisor, then the employer should be able to discover that information quickly and in more detail when reading your employment history.

I have found the simplest way to approach the compilation of a banner headline is to write down some key words describing previous roles. Your profile will no doubt be written many times before you arrive at the one that best describes your benefits to an employer. What is important is to be able to read the profile and be happy that it adequately sums up your strengths. Your profile is always written in the third party, that is, the way in which someone else would describe you.

Here are some examples of profiles to give you an idea how they should look:

A highly motivated and flexible sales manager with proven ability within the FMCG market. Has consistently achieved outstanding results in a customer-focused environment

An efficient and self-motivated administration manager who displays outstanding team-building skills. Has a highly versatile approach and a positive and enthusiastic manner

A highly effective and outstanding individual with substantial logistics and distribution experience, who has demonstrated considerable expertise in continuous improvement techniques by optimising performance and profitability within a change-oriented pan-European manufacturing environment

Skill matching

Before we begin to put together your CV let's take a look at skill matching. Skill matching is when you apply your CV towards a specific job. It is extremely easy to fall into the trap that once your CV is written it adopts a 'one size fits all' philosophy. This approach will make it much more difficult for an employer to pick out the key skills and achievements they are looking for and, as such, makes it less likely that you will be successful in your job applications. In a previous section we looked at the job-hunting zones where some areas are under your control and some areas are under the employer's. Remember, the CV zone is under *your* control and the more effort you put into this sector the better your end results will be.

The secret to moving from the job application stage to the interview stage is to obtain as much information as possible about the vacancy. Every employer has a 'wishlist' containing the key skills and experience the successful candidate will possess. Whatever the method used to advertise the vacancy the employer will have provided you with a series of clues about the candidate they are seeking to fill their position. It is simply a matter of identifying and logging these clues in order to focus your CV towards it.

On receipt of your CV the employer will scan your details to ascertain whether you have the necessary qualities they are looking for by matching your CV to the job. Make it easy for them by ensuring that your key skills and achievements stand out and are relevant. Remember – the key to getting an interview is to read the clues contained within the job description.

Let's take a look at a job advertisement and look for the clues the employer has provided to identify their ideal candidate.

Education representatives
Central Scotland

Jones and Brown, schoolbook publishers, are looking for intelligent, self-motivated and outgoing people for the above area to join our team of representatives.

These are challenging and interesting sales jobs with the country's top education publishers. It will involve visiting primary schools, mainly on appointment, to sell a wide range of outstanding and very popular classroom books.

You will need to have a good standard of education, a pleasant, confident manner, good organisational skills and some experience in speaking to groups. Previous sales experience, knowledge of educational issues and basic computer skills would be an advantage but we do provide excellent training. The position involves a significant amount of lifting and driving; therefore it is essential that you are fit and active. A company car, laptop computer and telephone will be provided.

By highlighting the key words used in the advert we can begin to identify a list of influencing factors that the employer will match against CVs (wishlist). When compiling a CV in response to this role it is essential to 'mirror' the words that the employer has used to ensure a 'match'.

I would recommend compiling a checklist by writing down the key words and phrases the employer has used and matching them against your skills and achievements. By following this exercise for every position you apply for you will ensure that your CV will be relevant to the role you are applying for and, more importantly, stand out from the crowd.

Let's take a look at an example of what a checklist could look like for the education representatives role:

Requirement	Match
Live within commuting distance of central Scotland	Live in Edinburgh
Have good standard of education	Educated to SCE higher grade
Have some knowledge of sales	Worked as a PA and liaised on a daily basis with the sales team on behalf of MD
Working on own initiative	Worked in an office on my own for 12 months and was required to be self-motivated and work on my own initiative
Pleasant and confident manner	While working as a PA I was required to have a pleasant and confident manner
Good organisational skills	Organised sales conferences, daily management of MD diary
Knowledge of education system	Have two daughters of primary school age
Experience of speaking to groups	Run Brownies two evenings a week
Computer skills	Fully conversant with MS Office packages
Fit and active	Hobbies are keep fit and tennis
Driving licence	Full clean licence since 1984

By compiling your details against the employers 'wishlist' you can ensure that you address each area within your CV and highlight your suitability to the employer. Ideally, you should attempt to achieve a match of around 80%

against the employers wishlist to ensure that your CV will attract initial interest at its first glance. Many people choose to apply for multiple vacancies in the belief that they have the ability to do the job irrespective of the skills the employer has asked for. This approach will result in a large volume of rejections and it can be extremely disheartening for the job hunter. I would strongly advise focusing all your efforts on jobs that match your skills and experience in order to make your job hunting a more fulfilling and profitable experience all round.

Before we move on to the next section why don't you choose a job advertisement from your local newspaper and identify the clues the employer has provided and compile them in a checklist.

Power words

Power words are an important aspect of your CV. Have a look at any job advertisement, whether on the internet or in your local newspaper, and you will very quickly identify the types of words that employers and agencies use to describe their ideal candidate. Deciding what words to use to highlight your skills and achievements can be made easier by following the employer's lead and using the mirroring process.

By mirroring the words the employer uses as well as adding powerful words of your own, you can ensure that your CV immediately catches the eye of the employer. You are in effect using the same words to describe yourself as the employer has used to describe their ideal candidate. Sounds too easy? It is – try it and see it work!

Words that could be used to describe your character include:

accomplished	accurate	adaptable	analytical	articulate
businesslike	capable	competitive	conscientious	cooperative
decisive	disciplined	efficient	energetic	enthusiastic
flexible	generous	honest	industrious	logical
meticulous	organised	perceptive	positive	reliable
self-confident	self-starting	tenacious	trustworthy	versatile

Words that could be used to expand and describe your skills and achievements include:

achieved	advised	analysed	accomplished	applied	assigned
budgeted	built	conducted	consolidated	constructed	coordinated
demonstrated	designed	delivered	developed	diagnosed	displayed
enabled	established	executed	expanded	facilitated	founded
gathered	generated	handled	headed	helped	implemented
improved	increased	influenced	initiated	instigated	investigated
launched	led	liaised	maintained	managed	measured
modified	motivated	negotiated	organised	outlined	overcame
performed	persuaded	presented	prioritised	produced	proposed
recommended	recruited	researched	revised	selected	structured
streamlined	supervised	trained	transformed	upgraded	verified

You might use some of the following power words to enhance your CV:

accurate	advanced	appointed	assertive	benefited
capably	challenging	communication	competently	consistent
counteracted	determination	decisive	diplomatic	enthusiastic
establish	experienced	expertise	flexible	gained
innovative	knowledge	motivate	potential	professional
rapidly	responsible	selected	significant	succeeded
tact	transferred	utilised	widened	won

CV layouts

There are three main CV layouts currently in use in the UK market:

- chronological CV
- functional CV
- combination CV.

Let's look at each one individually and identify which one best suits you.

Chronological CV

A chronological CV is the most commonly used type and the one that most people tend to stick to irrespective of circumstances. A chronological CV is a document that lists your employment history in reverse, i.e. starting at the present and working back. The benefits of using this type of CV is that it will highlight to an employer your career path to date in a fashion that makes it easy for them to pick out your key skills and achievements. Avoid this type of CV if you have an unstable work history or are trying to move away from the type of employment you are currently involved with.

John Smith

Address:	25 Glebe Street
	Glasgow G2 2PP
Contact details:	Tel 0141 555 5555
	Mob 0123 456789
	Email johnsmith@online.com

Profile

A highly effective and outstanding individual with substantial logistics and distribution experience, who has demonstrated considerable expertise in continuous improvement techniques by optimising performance and profitability within a change-oriented pan-European manufacturing and distribution environment.

Key skills

- Demonstrable track record of having achieved outstanding performance to strict timescales and budgetary targets
- Ability to liaise effectively at all levels
- Demonstrable track record in the implementation and ongoing review of KPIs within a fast moving distribution environment
- Over 15 years' experience at senior logistics management level

- Highly knowledgeable in the negotiation and implementation of logistical contractual arrangements on an international level

- Strong understanding of quality standards and health and safety procedures

Achievements

- Reduced inventory levels from six weeks to two resulting in a direct cost saving of £250K pa

- Negotiated agreement with HM Customs & Excise on import/export duty, resulting in direct cost saving of £175K pa

- Specially selected by Smith and Brown Engineering to form a working party to formulate and implement a harmonised inventory system resulting in improved communication and reporting structures internationally. International efficiency levels improved by at least 20% year on year

Career history

Warehouse Manager   *Smith and Brown Engineering*   *1988–present*

Reporting directly to the Senior Operations Manager, with complete accountability for the warehouse, shipping and transport from the main facilities in Scotland. The role involved the direct management of warehouse and distribution staff with a responsibility to ensure that strict KPI targets involving time and cost were met on a daily basis. Duties include:

- Management of all warehouse and distribution operations

- Liaising with HM Customs & Excise to ensure compliance with legislation, with particular focus on warehousing, duty relief and international freight

- Maintenance and development of internal and external client relationships across all levels

- Preparation and implementation of logistical forecasts while adhering to strict budgetary controls

- Complete responsibility for all movements and stock control from the facilities

- Focus on the ongoing evaluation of suppliers performance, transport lead times and financial liabilities

Key performance indicator parameters

- On time delivery (internal and external) – 95%

- Inventory control – strict two weeks' supply of raw materials

- Budgetary – £3.5m a year

Inventory Manager   Conney Distribution   1984–1988

Reporting directly to the Warehouse and Distribution Manager my responsibilities included:

- Management of international shipping office

- Complete inventory accountability

- Ownership of Customs & Excise relationship on behalf of Conney Distribution operations throughout the UK

Shipping Supervisor   N.P. Freight Forwarding   1978–1979
Shipping Clerk   Jones Shipping   1976–1978
Shipping Clerk   Barber and Co. Shipping   1972–1976

Training and development

European leadership practices

Change management

Continuous improvement processes

Diversity

IT skills – fully conversant with MS Office, MS Outlook

Personal summary

Date of birth:	25 October 1956
Driving licence:	Full/clean
Hobbies and interests:	Reading, walking, swimming

Functional CV

A functional CV is in a style that will emphasise your skills and achievements to an employer without being heavily biased towards a particular job role. The functional CV is ideal for individuals who may lack qualifications, have had different jobs that follow no clear line of progression or when you want to change your career completely and move in a new direction. By taking the employer's eye away from where you worked and what job you did, you can highlight your skills and achievements to suit the position you are applying for.

John Smith

Address:	12 Wraith Road
	London
	W1V 1XX
Contact details:	Tel 020 8123 456
	johnsmith@online.com

Profile

A committed, versatile, articulate and personable individual with a broad array of skills and experience. Highly motivated with a proven track record in a recruitment sales environment.

Objectives

To secure a position within a national recruitment organisation where my previous experience, sales and recruitment skills can be effectively utilised to maximise potential.

Key skills

- **Sales**. Responsibility for permanent sales within a busy recruitment organisation. Operating within a very competitive market consistently achieved and outperformed company sales targets. Grew business year on year by an average of 40%.

- **Communication**. Effectively liaised with clients and candidates across a broad range of business sectors. Held twice-yearly presentations at London University to attract graduates and was successful in placing 75% of the candidates registered with me. Presented to blue-chip clients on a regular basis and converted 1:3 to grow client base by 45% year on year.

- **Recruitment**. Formalised the recruitment process to ensure the best possible match between clients and candidates. Integrated this process into the London office and helped to improve sales figures across the division.

- **Management**. Managed a team of ten recruitment consultants across the permanent services sector and reduced staff turnover to an average of 7% from a previous high of 50%.

- **Business**. Responsibility to manage P&L accounts for the permanent services sector with the London branch. Prepared quarterly and annual projections presentation to board level. Achieved 40% growth year on year by developing business sectors and ensuring continuity within the business.

Career History

Divisional Manager	*Smith & Wyatt Consultancy*	*Jun 97–present*
Branch Manager	*Brown Smith & Co*	*Apr 92–Jun 97*
Branch Manager	*Rumble Bros*	*Jul 91–Apr 92*
Research Fellow	*Greengrass Insurance*	*Aug 87–Jul 91*

Education

Aug 84–Aug 87	Leeds University
	BSc (Hons) Chemistry

Personal details

Date of birth:	25 Oct 67
Driving licence:	Full/clean
Hobbies and interests:	Skiing, rally driving, football

Combination CV

A combination CV is designed to take the best from both the chronological and functional CV styles. It is often used where the individual wants to highlight their key skills as well as identifying their previous roles in order to give the employer a fuller picture of their capabilities. The drawback of combination CV is that it can tend to be long-winded and can have a detrimental effect during the initial scanning phase. I would recommend using this type of CV only if you are in a senior position and have an outstanding and solid employment background.

John Smith

Address:	12 Wraith Road
	London
	W1V 1XX
Contact details:	Tel: 020 8123 456
	johnsmith@online.com

Profile

A committed, versatile, articulate and personable individual with a broad array of skills and experience. Highly motivated with a proven track record in a recruitment sales environment.

Objectives

To secure a position within a national recruitment organisation where my previous experience, sales and recruitment skills can be effectively utilised to maximise potential.

Key skills

- **Sales**. Responsibility for permanent sales within an independent recruitment organisation. Operating within a very competitive market, consistently achieved and outperformed company sales targets.

- **Communication**. Effectively liaised with clients and candidates across a broad range of business sectors. Held twice-yearly presentations at London University to attract graduates and was successful in placing 75% of the candidates registered with me. Presented to blue-chip clients on a regular basis and converted 1:3 to grow client base by 45% year on year.

- **Recruitment**. Formalised the recruitment process to ensure the best possible match between clients and candidates. Integrated this process into the London office and helped to improve sales figures across the division.

- **Management**. Managed a team of ten recruitment consultants across the permanent services sector and reduced staff turnover to an average of 7% from a previous high of 50%.

- **Business**. Responsibility to manage P&L accounts for the permanent services sector with the London branch. Prepared quarterly and annual projections for presentation to board level.

Achieved 40% growth year on year by developing business sectors and ensuring continuity within the business.

Career history

Divisional Manager   Smith & Wyatt Consultancy Jun 97–present

Smith & Wyatt Consultancy is an independent recruitment organisation operating across 50 offices in the UK. Specialist divisions include insurance, accountancy and finance employing over 250 staff.

I reported directly to the group MD and include the following as major achievements:

- Growth of 40% pa since June 1998

- Team achievement of 75% placement rate against an industry average of 30%

- Introduced standard recruitment procedures across all divisions

Branch Manager Brown Smith & Co.   Apr 92–Jun 97

Brown Smith & Co. are insurance advisors to the recruitment industry.

I reported directly to the Sales Director and include the following as my major achievements:

- Restructuring of the entire sales division achieving cost savings of 12% pa

- Grew client base by 150% within 18 months of joining

- Recruitment and development of a team of eight sales consultants

Branch Manager Rumble Bros   Jul 91–Apr 92

Rumble Bros are independent financial advisors operating across the UK. Reporting to the Managing Partner, I was responsible for the growth and revenue generation to specific targets across the Greater London area. Achieved consistent individual results at least 25% above target every month.

Sales executive Greengrass Insurance   Aug 87–Jul 91

Greengrass Insurance are general household insurers based in Leeds. Reporting directly to the Branch Manager, I was responsible for the sale of household insurance within the Leeds area.

Education

Aug 84–Aug 87   Leeds University

                       BSc (Hons) Chemistry

Personal details

Date of birth: 25 Oct 67

Driving licence: Full/clean

Hobbies and interests: Skiing, rally driving, football

Dos and don'ts of CV writing

When deciding on the layout for your CV remember the following important factors to ensure that your CV is visually attractive:

Do ensure that margins are at least 2.5cm on all sides as this will give the CV an uncluttered first impression and keep you away from the temptation of trying to cram as much detail as possible into that sheet of A4 paper!

Do align your information to the left hand margin. Aligning your CV to the centre of the page or using pagination may look good in experienced hands, but for most of us I would suggest the left-hand margin. Remember that the eye reads from left to right so keep things simple to make a good first impression.

Do use common fonts and sizes. Especially important if applying for jobs online as some organisations will use computers to scan CVs at the point of entry. If your CV contains fonts the receiving computer does not recognise it may destroy your pride and joy before a human eye gets the chance to savour its delights!

Do use only one side of the paper. I know this is obvious to most of us – but it has been known!

Do keep sentences short and to the point to assist easy reading. If a document is easy to read it is much more likely to make the reader continue past the first page; don't be tempted to use large words where short words will do (if in doubt refer to the section on power words).

Do check spelling and grammar. Use your own and another individual's eye as well as the spellchecker on your computer. Your eye is far less likely to spot a spelling error you have made than another individual who is seeing it for the first time. Also, beware of computer spellcheckers, they are not foolproof and will not always spot bad grammar if the word is correctly spelt, i.e. 'they' instead of 'the'.

Do use high quality white paper. There is no need to spend a great deal of money on your paper but ensure that it portrays the impression you want to give, ideally it should be of 100gsm quality.

Don't fold or staple your CV. Your CV should arrive in pristine condition, so use an A4 sized envelope when despatching by post.

Don't underline key words. Use bold or shading to emphasise key areas or words.

Discrimination

Unfortunately, the screening process involved in any recruitment campaign involves people and with it, therefore, a degree of subjectivity. Whether you like it or not human beings have prejudices and as much as society has progressed over the years you may still encounter individuals who will make discriminatory assumptions based on the information contained in your CV. It is important when compiling your CV to be aware of any information that could affect your ability to progress to the interview stage. It is a matter of personal choice whether you choose deliberately to leave out information from your CV that could be used in a discriminatory manner; you may decide not to play into the hands of small-minded individuals and be understandably angry about having even to consider it. What is important to remember at this stage is that the individual who initially reads your CV may not be the person you would be working with and large organisations are likely to have very strict policies relating to any form of discrimination. I leave the choice up to you.

Let's take a look at the areas where you could potentially be discriminated against and discuss ways of overcoming them:

- ethnic origin
- gender
- sexuality
- age

- marital status
- health
- weight
- address
- education
- disability.

Remember to follow the key pointers of any CV, namely skills, achievements and relevance. By following this approach there are certain discriminatory areas that you could leave out of your CV such as marital status, sexuality, health, disability, education and weight.

The best approach to take if you feel that you may be discriminated against is deliberately to omit vital information and substitute it with an alternative.

Your name, for example, could provide details of your gender, so you could substitute your initials, e.g. A.M. Fagan gives no indication of my gender.

Your name, which may highlight your ethnic origin, could be substituted by its English version, i.e. Angelique Blanc replaced by Angela White. It is perfectly acceptable in the UK to use an alternative name as long as the reason for doing so is not illegal.

Taking the next step

'In one of the decisive battles of World War I, disastrous reports poured into the headquarters of Marshal Foch, the commander of the Allied Forces. The great general never lost heart. When things were at their worst, he drafted his famous order which is now in all textbooks of military strategy: "My center is giving way, my right is pushed back, my left is wavering. The situation is excellent. I shall attack!"'

James Keller

Sometimes we have to take a step back to look and see the direction we are heading in; our careers do not always take the path we want them to and you may feel that you have not achieved as much as you would have liked. The important thing to remember is that it is never too late to fulfil your dreams and if you are faced with obstacles you will find a way to overcome them. The compilation of a knockout CV is your first step towards achieving your goals and aspirations and finding the right job for you.

finding the
job

'If you believe you can, you probably can. If you believe you won't, you most assuredly won't. Belief is the ignition switch that gets you off the launching pad.'

Denis Waitley

3 Making a start

Planning your search

When you have compiled the information necessary for your CV it is natural that you should want to start applying for jobs straight away. I always recommend approaching this part of the process in the same way you would approach a project assigned to you in the workplace or at school/university.

The first place to start is to focus initially on a clear plan of attack by working out exactly how you are going to allocate your time and effort in sourcing the right sort of jobs for you. I find the best way to do this is to compile a job-hunting diary where you can set out your objectives and log all the information necessary to ensure you follow a clear and logical path. This is especially important if you are currently without a job or are due to face redundancy in the near future. Planning your time and focusing on the job hunt will greatly reduce the levels of stress you may encounter and keep you in a routine that will help to bolster your self-confidence. Irrespective of your circumstances you can alter the job-hunting diary to suit your time schedule and ensure that you record your activity and keep a focus on the whole process.

Example of a job-hunting diary

Day	AM	PM/evening
Monday	Buy local newspaper	Identify potential jobs
Tuesday	Visit job centre	Spend time on internet researching companies and visiting online job sites

Wednesday	Make contact with recruitment agencies and arrange to register	Network at tennis club
Thursday	Buy national newspapers	Identify potential jobs
Friday	Register with recruitment agencies	Customise CV to potential jobs identified this week and despatch in the post and via email

To further increase the effectiveness of the job-hunting diary I would also suggest that you create a new version for every week of your search. This will enable you to customise it depending on the time you have available to allocate that week, as well as recording overleaf the details of the jobs you have applied for and details of the recruitment agencies you have registered with.

Later in Part 2 we will look at the most common methods of finding advertised and unadvertised jobs, as well as providing you with a comprehensive list of the major UK job sites and UK newspapers carrying job advertisements. For now, let's look at some of the common abbreviations used in job advertisements.

Understanding employers' advertisements – what they say and what they mean

If you have been out of the job-hunting market for some time you may encounter unfamiliar abbreviations and terms used in job advertisements. Just like any topic there are fads and fashions that come and go with the times and keeping up with them can be a job in itself! I have compiled a list of some common abbreviations and words that you are likely to encounter together with what they mean.

£Salary+	Denotes that the salary indicated will be the starting point for negotiation depending on the skills and experience of the successful candidate
Agy	'Agency.' Recruitment agencies are required to indicate when advertising jobs that they are an agency and not an employer. This abbreviation will normally appear at the end of their advertisement
Benefits	Relates to items such as pension schemes, company cars, profit sharing etc.
Brown goods	Relates to items such as TVs, videos etc.
Circa (c)	Denotes where the salary will be in the region of, e.g. c£15,000 indicates the salary will be around £15,000 depending on the skills and experience of the successful candidate
Desirable	Denotes that the employer considers the experience or qualification, while not *essential*, to be desirable to the successful candidate
Essential	Denotes that the employer considers the experience or qualification to be essential to the successful candidate
Exp	'Experience'
FMCG	Fast moving consumer goods – often appears in sales-type positions and relates to an environment where there is a fast rotation of stock, e.g. foodstuffs
Grad	'Graduate'
K	'Thousands'. An abbreviation for thousands, e.g. £15K or £15,000
OTE	'On target earnings'. Normally seen alongside sales jobs and indicates that the salary is enhanced by earnings in relation to specific targets. The actual job may pay a basic salary of £12K, but the OTE is advertised as £22K as £10K is available to candidates who achieve their targets
PA	'Per annum.' Denotes the annual salary
Perm	'Permanent.' Used by recruitment agencies to describe permanent vacancies
PQ	'Part qualified.' Often found to describe accountancy jobs where the suitable candidate is deemed to have completed part of their full qualification
PQE	'Post-qualifying experience.' Denotes that suitable candidates should have some experience after gaining their qualification
Pro rata	'In proportion to.' Normally appears alongside a salary amount where the position is not full time, salary is taken as a proportion of the advertised salary dependent on the number of hours worked

PT	'Part time.' Denotes a part-time position
QBE	'Qualified by experience.' Often found in accountancy-type jobs where suitable candidates may have the skills and experience to do the role without possessing formal qualifications
Rec con	'Recruitment consultant.' An alternative to the use of 'agy'
Salary neg	'Salary negotiable.' Denotes that the salary of the successful candidate will be negotiable depending on skills and experience
Six-figure package	A salary of at least £100,000 a year
Temp	'Temporary.' Used by recruitment agencies to describe work of a temporary nature
VDU	'Visual display unit.' Denotes that the position will involve using a computer screen
White goods	Relates to items such as washing machines, dishwashers, cookers etc.
WP	'Word processing'

4 Recruitment consultants

Understanding recruitment consultants

The role of a recruitment consultant is perhaps one of the most misunderstood and under-utilised resources available to job hunters in the UK. In this chapter we will look at who they are, what they do and how to find the right one for you.

Recruitment agencies in the UK are part of a booming multi-billion pound industry covering a multitude of skills and experience across all sectors of the market. No matter what role you are seeking there will almost certainly be a recruitment organisation that can help you.

For the job hunter the recruitment industry is an invaluable tool, which should not be overlooked. Providing a wealth of experience with direct access to many unadvertised jobs and vital contacts across a range of industries, the right recruiter can save you time and effort and, more importantly, help you find the job that's right for you.

The recruitment industry makes its profit by a number of different methods dependent on the type of assignment. Briefly explained, recruitment organisations operating in the permanent market will charge their client a fee for finding and placing a suitable candidate in their vacancy, while recruitment organisations operating in the temporary marketplace will charge their client a fee based on an hourly rate. The important factor for job hunters to note is that they will not be charged for the agency's assistance or role in helping them to secure a new position.

Let's start by taking a look at the three main types of agency operating in the recruitment marketplace:

- high street recruitment
- specialist recruitment
- executive search recruitment.

These three operate within specific sectors of the market, often depending upon the type of employment you are seeking and the salary banding of that position.

Executive search recruitment

Normally operating at the top end of the market these companies, also known as headhunters, consist of recruiters paid by clients who hire them specifically to fill a position.

Organisations may find it impractical to advertise a vacancy openly in the media or the internet and often rely on executive search firms to tap into the market discreetly and identify suitable individuals.

Some executive search firms specialise in specific industries, while other generalist firms operate across a broad range of industries.

Executive search companies normally operate their fees in two different ways, retainer or on a contingency basis. Essentially, a retainer is when the client company hires an executive search company to search for a suitable candidate and is paid an agreed fee regardless of whether or not a suitable candidate is found. A contingency search fee is paid only when a candidate is hired. Fees are normally based on a percentage of the first year's salary including any benefits.

As an executive jobseeker you should be aware that executive search companies are working primarily on behalf of their clients and ensuring that their best interests are served; they are after all the paymasters! Your search for a new role may be a time-consuming business as executive search firms will concentrate on their current vacancies, ensuring they are filled before perhaps having the time to search out a role for you, the job hunter. For this reason you should approach a number of different search firms who are likely to have a number of different vacancies with numerous clients.

As a jobseeker, decide what firms you will approach – an initial telephone call will often indicate whether they can be of help to you.

For advice contact the Association of Executive Search Consultants at **www.aesc.org.**

Some organisations ask for your permission prior to sending your CV to an interested client, while others ask you to rely on their discretion as professionals. These types of search organisation are recommended for experienced professionals looking for their next career move, as they can offer advice, discretion and complete confidentiality that is vital in a high profile move.

High street recruitment

High street recruitment agencies are the types you would expect to come across while out shopping in your local town. They are normally identifiable by their appearance as shopfront locations and often advertise their current vacancies as part of the window display you would see as part of any high street store. Their vacancies tend to cover a range of difference jobs and are normally more driven by salary bracket (junior to £30k) than by individual specialisations.

High street agencies normally fall into one of two main categories:

- local
- national.

Local agencies are often part of a small branch network and are normally operated by local recruitment professionals. Local agencies have often been in the town for a number of years and as such they are likely to have built up a reputation and close business relationships with local companies. It is often the case that local high street agencies will have clients different from those at national high street agencies and it is worthwhile for the job hunter to register with both in order to reach a greater number of vacancies.

National high street agencies are identifiable by their presence in the high street; they tend to be recognisable by their brand names, for example Adecco, Manpower, Kelly Services. These types of agency operate in most major cities in the UK and have the added advantage to you, the jobhunter, by providing access to many national organisations operating at a local level.

Specialist recruitment

The main differences between high street and specialist agencies are their locations and the types of vacancies they deal with. Specialist agencies tend to operate within specific sectors of the market, for example IT or sales across a range of salary bands, and their locations tend to be in office-type blocks away from the hustle and bustle of the high street. In common with high street agencies, specialists fall into both local and national categories with similar advantages and disadvantages.

Getting the best out of your recruitment consultant

Over the years the role of a recruitment consultant has been derided and compared to that of an estate agent and the like. Whether this reputation is just and fair to either the recruitment consultant or estate agent is entirely a matter of opinion. I am sure we can all look back and identify good and bad in professions we have encountered in both our personal and working experiences; what is important to remember is that we should not tar all with the same brush.

In order to get the best out of your recruitment consultant it is important to understand their job and the priorities of their role in order to manage the situation to your advantage. The relationship you build up with your recruitment consultant will largely affect the outcome of your job-hunting success with them.

The hard and true fact of the matter is that a recruitment consultant, irrespective of the type of agency they are working for, is a sales person. This type of individual is driven by the need, each and every month to hit specific sales figures in accordance with targets set by their employer. A salesperson cannot and will not have the desire to help each and every person who walks through the doors of their agency, their main priority must always be to balance the needs of their clients against the availability of suitable candidates.

In order to provide a clear picture from both sides of the fence let's take a look at the common complaints directed against recruitment agencies and discuss the possible reasons behind them.

My consultant does not return my telephone calls

An extremely frustrating scenario that could be caused by a number of different possibilities. The important factor here is not to jump to conclusions and assume that they are avoiding you, it could be the case that they have not been passed the messages or that they are working to a deadline and have assigned time to return calls later. I would suggest leaving three messages for the consultant followed up by an email or letter asking them to get in touch. If this does not produce any results then spend your time registering with another agency that can help you with your job hunting.

I have seen a job advertised by my agency that fits my requirements. Why did they not call me?

Your recruitment consultant may have a number of reasons for advertising a vacancy where they already have a few suitable candidates, for example to reach a wider audience. I would recommend making contact with them to ascertain whether your skills and experience match up with the requirements of the role. This is especially important if you registered some time ago and they may have simply forgotten about you! Remember that the consultant cannot put every detail about the job in an advertisement and it may be the case on closer inspection that your skills do not exactly match the requirements detailed by the client.

My agency sent me along to an interview for a job that was completely unsuitable

It is essential to prepare for an interview irrespective of whether it is through an agency or not. Do not be pressurised into attending interviews unless you have received adequate information from your recruitment consultant. It is up to you as an individual to ask the questions that are important to you prior to attending any type of interview. If your recruitment consultant cannot provide you with the information then politely turn down the offer of an interview.

My CV was sent out to companies without my authorisation

Most reputable agencies will have a very strict protocol regarding the distribution of candidate CVs. It is important to discuss and agree with your recruitment consultant at the initial registration phase exactly what their policies are in order to give both you and the consultant a clear understanding of the expectations of both parties. If your CV has been sent out without your authorisation despite clear instructions to the contrary then make contact with the branch manager or directly to the organisation's head office to register your complaint. Be aware that, although you are perfectly within your rights to complain, you may well damage the relationship between you and the recruitment consultant.

I did not receive the correct wages while working as a temp

Each and every time you agree to work on a temporary assignment with an agency you should agree upfront with your consultant exactly how much you will be paid. If you fail to agree a pay rate then you could find yourself receiving far less than you thought without any real cause for complaint. Remember that the rate the agency quote you will be subject to tax and national insurance deductions by law, for example:

Pay rate agreed = £8.00 an hour

Hours worked = 40

Gross pay = £320.00

Less emergency tax = £67.20

Less NI = £20.00

Net pay = £232.80

If the rate you agreed with the agency is less than the gross hourly wage you have received then the first course of action would be a telephone call to your consultant as soon as you discover the error. Remember that almost all recruitment agencies require a signed timesheet in order to pay you, if you have not submitted a timesheet for whatever reason then make contact with your consultant without delay. If the outcome is not satisfactory then register your complaint with the branch manager or head office. Remember to have your facts clearly laid out in order to present your case in a professional manner.

I attended an interview through my agency and have not received any feedback

A good recruitment agency will prepare you thoroughly for a job interview and will provide you with interview feedback when received from the client. A good rule to stick to is to contact your recruitment consultant as soon as you have attended the interview to give them your thoughts and feelings on how the interview went. This will then provide them with sufficient information to contact the client and obtain their feedback. It may be the case that the client is waiting to see all candidates prior to providing their feedback and until this is received then the consultant cannot brief you. If the delay is more than two weeks without any real quantifiable reason then I would suggest moving on and finding another recruitment consultant who has some influence over their clients!

I sent my CV to your agency last week and haven't heard back from you

A busy successful agency could receive hundreds if not thousands of CVs every day via post and email. A perfect scenario would be to read every CV with interest and reply to every candidate – but in the real world that does not happen. If you forward your CV to an agency always follow it up with a telephone call within two days. That gives you a chance to speak directly with a consultant and ascertain whether or not they can assist you with your job hunting.

Every time I call your agency I speak to someone different

Many agencies have more than one person dealing with specific skills sectors making it likely that you will have more than one contact. The benefit to you as a job hunter is that more than one person has knowledge of you and your skills and when one consultant is unavailable it does not affect the continuity of service you receive.

I registered for temporary and permanent work, yet my agency only call me about temporary jobs

When you register for both temporary and permanent work it is likely that the consultant you see will have an interest in one specific sector. If they are a temporaries' consultant they will be more interested in placing you in temporary assignments as that is the way they make money for themselves! If you have not met with or spoken to the permanent consultant it is unlikely that they will think of you when a suitable position becomes available. Make an appointment to discuss your requirements with them to ensure your desires are achieved.

I have registered with lots of agencies by sending my CV but they have not got back to me

The majority of agencies in the UK marketplace will consider you to be registered with them for work only when you have completed a formal registration process, which normally entails a face-to-face interview. Despatching your CV to an agency and then assuming you are registered is a common mistake that many job hunters make. As previously discussed follow up your CV with a telephone call and arrange to meet with a consultant.

My consultant will not put me forward for a job that I know will suit my skills and experience

Your consultant has been briefed by the client company on the skills and experience as well as personality type that will suit their particular role. It is then the consultant's job to match up suitable applicants. Trust your consultants' judgement – this is the individual the client has trusted to forward only suitable candidates and you may not be privy to all the information.

Dos and don'ts of dealing with recruitment consultants

Do work out exactly what you want prior to registering with any agency. Often candidates will make contact with an agency with no clear idea of where their career aspirations lie and hope that the consultant can point them in the right direction. As previously discussed, the aim of a recruitment consultant is to place candidates in jobs in order to fulfil specific targets, very few of them will have the time to devote to candidates requiring career counselling. Equally, if you do not feel that the consultant is asking you the right questions then volunteer the information, as the more your consultant knows about you and where you want to go the more likely that they will be able to assist you to find your next job role.

Do focus on building a relationship with your consultant as it will help both you and them to identify the right roles for you. Relationships are always best conducted either face to face or by telephone, it helps to put a human angle on things and will develop much better than an email relationship.

Do register with more than one agency when conducting your job search. Ideally you should aim to register with around three to ensure that you are not focusing all your hopes and dreams on one individual and are more likely to get a selection of vacancies. Do not be tempted to register with every agency in town as this can very quickly become counterproductive as a consultant is less likely to go the extra mile for you if you have 20 other consultants working on your behalf. When deciding which agencies to approach have a look in your local newspaper and see who is advertising jobs in your profession or take a look in the yellow pages or online to build up a picture of the type of agencies suitable to your needs.

Do be honest with your consultant especially if you have registered with other agencies or have interviews arranged with companies. In line with the relationship-building process both you and your consultant should feel that information is being shared for the common good. If you withhold information your consultant could feel justified in treating you cautiously.

Do take your consultant's advice. On matters such as salary expectations or career aspirations your consultant is the person best placed to provide you with a realistic overview of the current market situation.

Do keep in touch with your consultant. A telephone call once each week, or as advised by them, is more than sufficient. Don't be tempted to pester them with telephone calls in the hope that they will focus all their efforts on you alone; it could have the opposite effect.

Do ask your consultant for advice on your CV. Most quality recruitment agencies will retype your CV in a format chosen by them prior to presentation to a client, however, it would be prudent to seek advice on the information and quality of your CV directly from them in the event that you choose to conduct your own job hunting.

Do ensure that you receive coaching from your consultant prior to attending any interviews with clients. Ask how you come across and if there are any hints and tips you could use to ensure a more polished performance.

Do insist on being notified before your CV is distributed to clients. This will ensure that you can keep some control over the situation and inform your other agency contacts to avoid a conflict of interests. Many agencies will only agree to providing details on their clients once your CV has been despatched; remember it is a competitive market and they could be in direct competition with other agencies you have registered with.

Do attend an interview with a recruitment agency dressed as you would for a 'real' interview. Recruitment consultants will form an opinion of and make decisions on your suitability for presentation to their clients based on their interview with you. If you turn up looking scruffy and ill-prepared you are likely to create the wrong impression and could directly affect your chances of proceeding any further with them.

Do keep in contact with your recruitment consultant even after you have been successful in your job hunting, whether it was through them or not. A card or letter thanking them for their interest will ensure that the door stays open if you need them again in the future.

Don't attempt to contact an agency client directly. The agency has been directed by the employer to handle specific stages of the process and it would be extremely bad form on your part to attempt to take control of the situation. Remember that your consultant will do everything in their power to ensure a successful outcome; after all, they are looking after your interests as well as the clients.

Don't attempt to bully or harass your consultant in order to be put forward for a job they think you are unsuitable for. The likely outcome is going to be your having to find another recruitment consultant.

Don't be persuaded to attend an interview without sufficient information about the vacancy. Some recruitment consultants may be targeted to achieve a set amount of interviews each week and will be keen to send you whether you fit the requirements of the role or not.

Don't attempt to play one agency off against another. The recruitment industry is a very close-knit community and you will quickly gain a bad reputation that could adversely affect your chances of using them to help you find your next role.

Don't burn your bridges with a recruitment consultant. If you are unsatisfied about a particular part of your relationship with them or have managed to get a new job without their help always keep the lines of communication open and conduct them in a professional manner. After all, you never know when you might come across them again in the future.

Recruitment industry professional bodies

The recruitment industry is operated in accordance with the Employment Agencies Act 1973 and although the industry is no longer licensed all companies operating within this sector must operate in accordance with this act.

The majority of agencies operating within the recruitment market belong to at least one professional body depending on their type of business. To help you find the recruitment business that would best serve your needs or indeed if you have any complaints about recruitment agencies that cannot be resolved by approaching them directly you may wish to contact the relevant professional body for advice.

Professional body	Description	Contact
Association of Executive Search Consultants (AESC)	A worldwide professional association representing executive search consultants	www.aesc.org
Association of Online Recruiters (AOLR)	Part of the Recruitment and Employment Confederation, set up specfically to promote the highest ethical standards among its members	www.aolr.org
Association of Search and Selection Consultants (ASSC)	Part of the Recruitment and Employment Confederation, representing recruitment firms operating within the search and selection marketplace	assc@rec.uk.com
Association of Technology Staffing Companies (ATScO)	Representing companies operating within the technology staffing industry	www.atsco.org
Recruitment and Employment Confederation (REC)	The largest recruitment industry body with membership of over 6,000 organisations within the recruitment market	www.rec.uk.com

5 Online recruitment

A recent survey by Oftel discovered that over 11 million homes in the UK have internet access. It is therefore not surprising to discover that over 50% of UK companies now use online recruitment as part of their strategy for attracting workers. If you are a serious job hunter, you cannot ignore the internet. Use it as a valuable resource for sourcing vacancies and conducting your company research.

Finding the job site for you

With the number of UK job sites growing every day it is often difficult to decide which one is right for you, how many you should register with and – for the first-time user – understanding how they work.

Briefly, there are a multitude of job sites available on the internet servicing the UK marketplace roughly categorised as follows:

- industry specific, e.g. IT jobs
- skill specific, e.g. SAP programmers
- location specific, e.g. jobs in Scotland
- recruitment agency specific, e.g. Adecco
- company specific, e.g. IBM.

With such a wide array to choose from it is little wonder that many of us can become confused when embarking on our job search. To further add to the confusion you will discover, as I did, that many sites share jobs, which can become a little frustrating when attempting to identify which site is best suited to your needs.

When choosing who to place their vacancies with, employers and recruitment agencies will often look at the number of vacancies in their specific sector as well as the proportion of overall traffic visiting the site before choosing the site that will attract the type of individual they are looking for to fill their job roles. The number and type of jobs carried on a site is a useful indicator of their relevance to you the job hunter in deciding whether or not to register with them.

The Association of Online Recruiters (AOLR) is an industry body established by online recruitment companies that aims to regulate the online recruitment industry. Membership requires all sites to adhere to a code of ethical conduct that includes a commitment to the security of a candidate's personal information and the provision of meaningful traffic figures to advertisers. If you are embarking into online recruitment for the first time I would suggest that you only register with sites that are members of AOLR to give you added confidence in their professional conduct. That said, there are many reputable and very successful sites that have chosen, for whatever reason, *not* to join AOLR, while still conducting their affairs in a highly professional manner.

How do online job sites operate?

In general the job sites operating in the UK marketplace will offer varying levels of service including:

- CV posting
- personal job search agent with email notification
- CV management
- message boards
- privacy options
- expert advice on job hunting from resident career counsellors
- newsletters.

As a job hunter you can decide how many or how few of the services on offer you want to use. If, for example, you are looking for a new job while still employed it would be wise to consider whether or not to post your CV onto the site (dangerous if your current employer happens also to use the site). The privacy options included on many of the sites will give you control over exactly what happens to your details after registration.

Most large organisations in the UK market will have their own website, specifically designed to provide information on their organisation as well as providing details of any vacancies. If there is a specific company you are interested in it would be wise to view their website in order to gain a fuller understanding of their business. If you do not have a web address then use a search engine to help you find it. I recommend **www.google.co.uk** which, in my opinion, is one of the best available.

Applying for jobs online

Before you start job hunting online ensure that you have a copy of your CV available on your computer or on a floppy disc. Many sites offer a facility to compile a CV on your behalf using their software. I would always advise using your own well-thought-out and researched CV to create a more powerful document. It also gives you the advantage of standing out among the other people using that site who have chosen to use a predetermined format. As discussed earlier in the section on CVs ensure that yours is aligned each and every time to the job you are applying for in order to highlight your key skills and achievements and, more importantly, focus the employer's eye on your suitability. If you are not applying for a specific job but intending to post your CV online for employers to see, then spend some time researching the common skills and phrases that employers use to describe the type of role you desire and use that same language in your CV.

Employers and recruitment agencies are increasingly using software designed to screen applications for identifiable key words relating to the advertised role as well as trawling job boards for suitable candidates. Before replying to an advertised post or posting your CV onto a job board take some time out to consider the language that is used by employers and agencies when seeking someone with similar skills. It is especially important to use the identified key words to increase your chances of web screening software isolating your details among your fellow job hunters.

When you have identified a job that fulfils your criteria it is as easy as following the instructions on screen to make your application directly to the employer or the recruitment agency. The instructions will normally guide you to your email screen and ask you to enclose your CV as an attachment to the main document.

Dos and don'ts of email etiquette

Email etiquette is often harder to judge when deciding what information to include in your covering letter/email. Email has now become such a norm when communicating with family and friends that many people fall into the trap of becoming overly familiar when using email to apply for jobs. Think of an email when used in conjunction with a job application in exactly the same way as you would a hard copy covering letter.

Do check your email for spelling and grammatical errors – use a spellchecker if you have one. Remember to ensure that grammar is appropriate to the country you are applying to, e.g. UK English, US English.

Do ensure that you reread your email and covering document prior to hitting the send button. Their very convenience of speed can also be their downfall, as no sooner have you hit the send button than your eye catches a glaring mistake as it winds its way to your intended recipient

Do be concise. Ensure that your message conveys your point; long emails can be boring and irritating for the reader.

Do ensure that your email address is professional. Names such as HotDan99@freemail.com or guesswho@freemail.com are likely to be viewed not only as unprofessional but potential virus carriers that may be deleted on receipt.

Do include a subject box. Always complete this box, as it will indicate to the recipient straight away which position you are applying for. An email that arrives with 'No Subject' may never be opened as it does not indicate its subject and could be viewed as spam.

Do ensure that the main eye-catching detail of your email is contained within the screen window. You only have one chance to sell yourself and the recipient may not bother to scroll down their screen to read the part where your information starts to get interesting.

Don't include photographs with your email. In my opinion, photographs are never a good idea when used in conjunction with job applications as they can be used in a discriminatory manner, but their main failing when transmitted by email is that they are likely to hit a firewall installed by the intending company and may be deleted on receipt.

Don't use abbreviations that may make perfect sense to you but leave your addressee in complete bewilderment.

Don't write in capital letters. It amounts to shouting at your recipient!

Don't use fancy fonts or different coloured backgrounds in your email. Keep to a business format using a recognised business font, e.g. Times New Roman.

Online job sites

For a comprehensive list of job sites servicing the UK market, please visit www.business-minds.com/goto/brilliantjobhunter. These sites have been chosen based on their ease of use, market penetration and popularity among UK jobseekers.

6 Newspapers and trade publications

Prior to the boom in internet job posting, newspapers and trade publications were the traditional forms for advertising jobs in the UK marketplace. Despite the success of online posting many companies still continue to use these traditional methods, which work every bit as successfully as, if not more so than, online posting and advertising.

As a serious job hunter you should ensure that you continue to use this method for sourcing jobs in order to cast your net as widely as possible.

Trade publications are invaluable to job hunters in specific market sectors as they allow you the opportunity to focus on job advertisements appropriate to your skills and experience as well as providing valuable news on the latest happenings within your industry.

Newspapers

The following is a listing of all of the major UK newspapers operating across the length and breadth of the UK and Northern Ireland to help you to identify the publication that best suits your needs.

Nationwide

Newspaper	Web address	Primary market
Daily Mail	www.dailymail.co.uk	Nationwide
Daily Telegraph	www.telegraph.co.uk	Nationwide
Financial Times	www.ft.com	Nationwide
Guardian	www.guardianunlimited.co.uk	Nationwide
Independent	www.independent.co.uk	Nationwide
Mail on Sunday	www.mailonsunday.co.uk	Nationwide
Mirror	www.mirror.co.uk	Nationwide
Sunday Mirror	www.sundaymirror.co.uk	Nationwide
Sunday Telegraph	www.sundaytelegraph.co.uk	Nationwide
Sunday Times	www.sunday-times.co.uk	Nationwide
The Observer	www.observer.co.uk	Nationwide
The Times	www.the-times.co.uk	Nationwide

East Midlands

Daventry Express	www.daventryonline.co.uk	Daventry
Derby Evening Telegraph	www.chesterfieldtoday.co.uk	Derby
Derbyshire Times	www.chesterfieldtoday.co.uk	Chesterfield
Eastwood and Kimberley Advertiser	www.eastwoodtoday.co.uk	Eastwood
Hucknall and Bulwell Dispatch	www.hucknalltoday.co.uk	Hucknall
Ilkeston Advertiser	www.ilkestontoday.co.uk	Ilkeston
Leicestershire Mercury	www.thisisleicestershire.co.uk	Leicester
Lincolnshire Echo	www.thisislincolnshire.co.uk	Lincolnshire
Mansfield Chronicle	www.mansfieldtoday.co.uk	Mansfield
Matlock Mercury	www.matlocktoday.co.uk	Matlock
Northampton Chronicle & Echo	www.northamptonchronicleecho.co.uk	Northampton
Northamptonshire Evening Telegraph	www.northamptonshireeveningtelegraph.co.uk	Northamptonshire
Nottingham Evening Post	www.thisisnottingham.co.uk	Nottingham

| Rutland Post | www.rutnet.co.uk/customers/rutlandtimes | Rutland |
| Worksop Guardian | www.worksoptoday.co.uk | Worksop |

Eastern counties

Bury Free Press	www.buryfreepress.co.uk	Bury St Edmunds
Cambridge Evening News	www.cambridge-news.co.uk	Cambridge
East Anglian Daily Times	www.suffolk-now.co.uk	Ipswich
Eastern Daily Press	www.norfolk-now.co.uk	Norwich
Essex Chronicle	www.thisisessex.co.uk	Essex
Evening Gazette	www.thisisessex.co.uk	Colchester
Evening News	www.norfolk-now.co.uk	Norwich
Evening Star	www.eveningstar.co.uk	Ipswich
Evening Telegraph	www.peterboroughnet.co.uk	Peterborough
Hemel Hempstead Gazette	www.hemelonline.co.uk	Hemel Hempstead
Luton and Dunstable Herald and Post	www.lutononline.co.uk	Luton and Dunstable
Lynn News	www.lynnnews.co.uk	King's Lynn
Newark Advertiser	www.newarkadvertiser.co.uk	Newark
St Albans and Harpenden Observer	www.stalbansobserver.co.uk	St Albans
Watford Observer	www.watfordobserver.co.uk	Watford

Greater London

Guardian Weekly	www.guardianunlimited.co.uk	London
Hampstead and Highgate Express	www.hamhigh.co.uk	Hampstead and Highgate
London Evening Standard	www.thisislondon.co.uk	London
Newham Recorder	www.newhamrecorder.co.uk	Newham
Newsquest London Newspapers	www.thisislondon.co.uk	London
South London Press	www.southlondononline.co.uk	South London
Weekend City Press Review	www.news-review.co.uk	London
The Metro	www.metro.co.uk	London

Northeast and West England

Newspaper	Web address	Primary market
Berwick Advertiser	www.tweeddalepress.co.uk	Berwick
Blackburn Citizen	www.thisislancashire.co.uk	Blackburn
Blackpool Citizen	www.thisislancashire.co.uk	Blackpool
Blackpool Gazette	www.blackpoolonline.co.uk	Blackpool
Bolton Evening News	www.thisislancashire.co.uk	Bolton
Burnley Citizen	www.thisislancashire.co.uk	Burnley
Bury Times	www.thisislancashire.co.uk	Bury
Chorley Citizen	www.thisislancashire.co.uk	Chorley
Chronicle Newspapers	www.icchesteronline.co.uk	Chester
Congleton Guardian	www.thisiswirral.co.uk	Congleton
Crewe Guardian	www.thisischeshire.co.uk	Crewe
Cumberland and Westmorland Herald	www.cwherald.com	Cumberland and Westmorland
Cumberland News	www.cumberland-news.co.uk	Cumberland
East Lancs News	www.eastlancnews.co.uk	East Lancs
Evening Chronicle	www.evening-chronicle.co.uk	Newcastle upon Tyne
Gateshead Post	www.gateshead-post.co.uk	Gateshead
Herald and Post	www.herald-and-post.co.uk	Newcastle upon Tyne
Isle of Man News	www.isle-of-man-newspapers.com	Isle of Man
Knutsford Guardian	www.thisiswirral.co.uk	Knutsford
Lancashire Evening Post	www.lep.co.uk	Lancashire
Lancashire Evening Telegraph	www.thisislancashire.co.uk	Lancashire
Lancaster Citizen	www.thisislancashire.co.uk	Lancaster
Lancaster Guardian	www.lancasteronline.co.uk	Lancaster
Leigh Journal	www.thisislancashire.co.uk	Leigh
Liverpool Daily Post	www.icliverpool.icnetwork.co.uk	Liverpool
Liverpool Echo	www.liverpool.com/echo	Liverpool
Manchester Evening News	www.manchesteronline.co.uk	Manchester
Morecambe Visitor News	www.morecambeonline.co.uk	Morecambe

News and Star	www.news-and-star.co.uk	Carlisle
North Cumberland Times and Star	www.times-and-star.co.uk	North Cumberland
North East Evening Gazette	www.icteeside.co.uk	Middlesbrough
North West Evening Mail	www.nwemail.co.uk	Barrow in Furness
Northern Echo	www.thisisthenortheast.co.uk	Darlington
Northwich Guardian	www.thisiswirral.co.uk	Northwich
Ormskirk Magull and Skelmersdale Advertiser	www.ormskirkadvertiser.co.uk	Ormskirk
Preston Citizen	www.thisislancashire.co.uk	Preston
Runcorn World	www.thisiswirral.co.uk	Runcorn
Sale and Altrincham Messenger	www.thisisstrafford.co.uk	Sale and Altrincham
Southport Visiter	www.southportvisiter.co.uk	Southport
St Helens Star	www.thisislancashire.co.uk	St Helens
Stretford and Urmston Messenger	www.thisisstrafford.co.uk	Stretford
Sunderland Echo	www.sunderland-echo.co.uk	Sunderland
The Journal	www.thejournal.co.uk	Newcastle upon Tyne
The Metro	www.metro.co.uk	Manchester and Newcastle
Westmorland Gazette	www.thisisthelakedistrict.co.uk	Westmorland
Whitehaven News	www.whitehaven-news.co.uk	Whitehaven
Widnes World	www.thisiswirral.co.uk	Widnes
Wigan Observer	www.wiganonline.co.uk	Wigan
Winsford Guardian	www.thisiswinsford.co.uk	Winsford
Wirral Globe	www.thisiswirral.co.uk	Wirral

Northern Ireland

Alpha Group Newspapers	www.ulsternet-ni.co.uk	Northern Ireland
The Belfast Telegraph	www.belfasttelegraph.co.uk	Belfast
The Fermanagh Herald	www.fermanaghherald.com	Fermanagh
The Impartial Reporter	www.impartialreporter.com	Fermanagh
The Irish News	www.irishnews.com	Ireland
The Ulster Herald	www.ulsterherald.com	Ulster

Wales

Newspaper	Web address	Primary market
Denbighshire Free Press	www.denbighshirefreepress.co.uk	Denbighshire
Evening Leader	www.eveningleader.co.uk	Wrexham
Flintshire Leader	www.flintshirestandard.co.uk	Flintshire
Oswestry and Border Counties Advertiser	www.bordercountiesadvertiser.co.uk	Oswestry and border counties
Powys County Times	www.countytimes.co.uk	Powys
The Bangor Chronicle	www.northwaleschronicle.co.uk	Bangor
The Llanelli Star	www.tindlenews.co.uk	Llanelli
The North Wales Chronicle	www.northwaleschronicle.co.uk	North Wales
The North Wales Pioneer	www.northwalespioneer.co.uk	North Wales
The Pioneer	www.thisissouthwales.co.uk	South Wales
The Rhyl Journal	www.rhyljournal.co.uk	Rhyl
The South Wales Evening Post	www.thisissouthwales.co.uk	South Wales
The Western Mail and Echo	www.totalwales.com	Wales
Ycymro	www.y-cymro.co.uk	Welsh national

Scotland

Scotland on Sunday	www.scotlandonsunday.com	Scotland
Scottish and Universal Newspapers	www.inside-scotland.co.uk	Scotland
The Aberdeen and District Independent	www.aberdeen-indy.co.uk	Aberdeen
The Aberdeen Press and Journal	www.thisisnorthscotland.co.uk	Aberdeen
The Courier	www.thecourier.co.uk	Dundee
The Daily Record	www.record-mail.co.uk	Scotland
The Dunoon Observer	www.dunoon-observer.co.uk	Dunoon
The Evening Telegraph	www.eveningtelegraph.co.uk	Dundee
The Evening Times	www.eveningtimes.co.uk	Glasgow
The Falkirk Herald	www.falkirkherald.co.uk	Falkirk
The Fife Free Press	www.fifefreepress.co.uk	Fife region
The Hawick News	www.hawick-news.co.uk	Hawick

The Herald	www.theherald.co.uk	Scotland
The Metro	www.metro.co.uk	Glasgow and Edinburgh
The Scotsman	www.scotsman.com	Scotland
The Shetland Times	www.shetlandtoday.co.uk	Shetland
The Southern Reporter	www.tweeddalepress.co.uk	Borders
The Stornoway Gazette	www.stornowaygazette.co.uk	Stornoway
The Sunday Herald	www.sundayherald.com	Scotland
The Sunday Mail	www.record-mail.co.uk	Scotland
The Sunday Post	www.sundaypost.com	Scotland

Southeast England

Banbury Guardian	www.banburyguardian.co.uk	Banbury
Bexhill Observer	www.bexhillobserver.co.uk	Bexhill
Buckingham Advertiser	www.buckinghamonline.co.uk	Buckingham
Bucks Free Press	www.thisisbuckinghamshire.co.uk	Buckingham
Bucks Herald	www.bucksherald.co.uk	Buckingham
Chichester Observer	www.chiobserver.co.uk	Chichester
Courier	www.thisiskentandeastsussex.co.uk	Kent and East Sussex
Dimbleby Newspapers	www.dimbleby.co.uk	Dimbleby
Dorking Advertiser	www.dorkingadvertiser.co.uk	Dorking
East Grinstead Observer	www.eastgrinsteadobserver.co.uk	East Grinstead
Eastbourne Herald	www.eastbourneherald.co.uk	Eastbourne
Epsom and Banstead Herald	www.epsomherald.co.uk	Epsom and Banstead
Evening Argus	www.thisisbrighton.co.uk	Brighton
Evening Echo	www.thisisessex.co.uk	Basildon
Hampshire Chronicle	www.thisishampshire.net	Winchester
Isle of Wight County Press	www.thisishampshire.net	Isle of Wight
Leatherhead Advertiser	www.leaderheadadvertiser.co.uk	Leatherhead
Maidenhead Advertiser	www.maidenhead-advertiser.co.uk	Maidenhead
Mid Sussex Times	www.midsussextimes.co.uk	Mid Sussex
Milton Keynes Citizen	www.mkcitizen.co.uk	Milton Keynes

Newspaper	Web address	Primary market
Newbury Weekly News	www.newburynews.co.uk	Newbury
Oxford Mail	www.thisisoxford.co.uk	Oxford
Reading Chronicle	www.readingchronicle.co.uk	Reading
Sevenoaks Chronicle	www.thisiskentandeastsussex.co.uk	Sevenoaks
Slough and Langley Observer	www.thisisslough.com	Slough and Langley
Southern Daily Echo	www.dailyecho.co.uk	Southampton
Surrey Advertiser	www.surreyad.co.uk	Surrey
Surrey Mirror	www.surreymirror.co.uk	Surrey
Sussex Express	www.sussexexpress.co.uk	Sussex
The News	www.thenews.co.uk	Portsmouth
West Sussex County Times	www.horshamonline.co.uk	Horsham
Worthing Herald	www.worthingherald.co.uk	Worthing

Southwest England

Bath Chronicle	www.thisisbath.com	Bath
Bristol Evening Post	www.epost.co.uk	Bristol
Citizen	www.thisisgloucestershire.co.uk	Gloucester
Clarion	www.clarion-news.co.uk	Yeovil
Cornish Guardian	www.thisiscornwall.co.uk	Cornwall
Cornish Weekly News	www.thisiscornwall.co.uk	Cornwall
Evening Advertiser	www.thisiswiltshire.co.uk	Wiltshire
Evening Herald	www.thisisplymouth.co.uk	Plymouth
Express and Echo	www.thisisexeter.co.uk	Exeter
Gazette and Herald	www.thisiswiltshire.co.uk	Wiltshire
Gloucestershire Echo	www.thisisgloucestershire.co.uk	Gloucestershire
Guernsey Evening Press	www.guernsey-press.com	Guernsey
Herald Express	www.thisissouthdevon.co.uk	South Devon
Jersey Evening Post	www.jerseyeveningpost.com	Jersey
Mid Devon Gazette	www.middevongazette.co.uk	Mid Devon
North Devon Journal	www.thisisnorthdevon.co.uk	North Devon

Swindon Business News	www.swindon-business.net	Swindon
Taunton Times	www.thisistaunton.co.uk	Taunton
Wellington Weekly News	www.thisisnorthdevon.co.uk	Wellington
Western Daily Press	www.westpress.co.uk	Bristol
Western Gazette	www.westgaz.co.uk	Yeovil
Western Morning News	www.westernmorningnews.co.uk	Plymouth
Wiltshire Times	www.thisiswiltshire.co.uk	Wiltshire

West Midlands

Birmingham Post and Mail	www.go2birmingham.co.uk	Birmingham
Bromsgrove Advertiser	www.thisisworcestershire.co.uk/worcs.bromsg	Bromsgrove
Coventry Evening Telegraph	www.go2coventry.co.uk	Coventry
Dudley News	www.thisistheblackcountry.co.uk	Dudley
Evesham Journal	www.thisisworcestershire.co.uk/worcs/evesham	Evesham
Express and Star	www.westmidlands.com	West Midlands
Halesowen News	www.thisistheblackcountry.co.uk	Halesowen
Hereford Times	www.thisishereford.co.uk	Hereford
Kenilworth Weekly News	www.kenilworthonline.co.uk	Kenilworth
Kidderminster Shuttle	www.thisisworcestershire.co.uk/worcs/kidder	Kidderminster
Leamington Spa Courier	www.leamingtononline.co.uk	Leamington
Ludlow Advertiser	www.newsquestmidlands.co.uk/ludlow	Ludlow
Malvern Gazette and Ledbury Reporter	www.thisisworcestershire.co.uk/worcs/malvern	Malvern and Ledbury
Redditch Advertiser	www.thisisworcestershire.co.uk/worcs/redditch	Redditch
Rugby Advertiser	www.rugbyonline.com	Rugby
Sentinel	www.thisisstafford.co.uk	Stafford
Shropshire Star	www.shropshire-on-line.com	Shropshire
Stourbridge News	www.thisistheblackcountry.co.uk	Stourbridge
Stratford Herald	www.stratford-herald.co.uk	Stratford upon Avon
The Metro	www.metro.co.uk	Birmingham
Warwick Courier	www.warwickonline.co.uk	Warwick
Worcester Evening News	www.thisisworcester.co.uk	Worcester

Yorkshire and Humberside

Newspaper	Web address	Primary market
Barnsley Chronicle	www.barnsley-chronicle.co.uk	Barnsley
Craven Herald	www.cravenherald.co.uk	Skipton
Dewsbury Reporter	www.dewsburyonline.co.uk	Dewsbury
Doncaster Free Press	www.doncasteronline.co.uk	Doncaster
Evening Press	www.thisisyork.co.uk	York
Goole Times	www.btinternet.com/gooletimes	Goole
Grimsby Evening Telegraph	www.thisisgrimsby.co.uk	Grimsby
Harrogate Advertiser	www.harrogate-advertiser-series.co.uk	Harrogate
Huddersfield Daily Examiner	www.ichuddersfield.co.uk	Huddersfield
Hull Daily Mail	www.thisishull.co.uk	Hull
Ilkley Gazette	www.ilkleygazette.co.uk	Ilkley
Keighley News	www.keighleynews.co.uk	Keighley
Scunthorpe Evening Telegraph	www.thisisscunthorpe.co.uk	Scunthorpe
Star	www.sheffweb.co.uk	Sheffield
Telegraph and Argus	www.thisisbradford.co.uk	Bradford
The Metro	www.metro.co.uk	Leeds and Sheffield
Wharfedale Observer	www.wharfedaleobserver.co.uk	Wharfedale
Yorkshire Evening Post	www.yorkshire-evening-post.co.uk	Yorkshire
Yorkshire Post	www.ypn.co.uk	Yorkshire

Trade publications

There are a multitude of trade publications covering the UK marketplace. The following is a listing of the most popular among UK job hunters.

Publication	Web address	Target industry
Accountancy Age	www.accountancyage.co.uk	Accountancy
Accountancy Magazine	www.accountancymag.co.uk	Accountancy
British Medical Journal	www.bmj.com	Healthcare
Campaign	www.campaignlive.com	Advertising
Chemist and Druggist	www.dotpharmacy.co.uk	Pharmaceutical
Chemistry and Industry	www.chemind.org	Scientific
Civil Engineers	www.nceplus.co.uk	Civil engineering
Computer Weekly	www.computerweekly.co.uk	IT/telecom
Construction	www.cnplus.co.uk	Construction
Construction Plus	www.constructionplus.co.uk	Construction
Current Archaeology	www.archaeology.co.uk	Archaeology
Electronic Time	www.electronictimes.com	Electronics
Electronics	www.ebtmag.com	Electronics
Electronics Weekly	www.electronicsweekly.co.uk	Electronics/engineering
Environmental	www.ifi.co.uk	Environmental
Environmental Data Services	www.ends.co.uk	Environmental
Financial Director	www.financialdirector.co.uk	Accountancy and finance
FleetNews	www.automotive.co.uk	Automotive
Food Manufacture	www.thefoodsite.com	Food and drink
Health Service Journal	www.hsj.co.uk	Healthcare
Housing Today	www.housingtoday.org.uk	Housing
In Brief	www.inbrief.co.uk	Legal
Insurance Times	www.insurancetimes.co.uk	Insurance
Journalism	www.journalism.co.uk	Journalism
Language International	www.language-international.com	Language; multilingual
Leisure and Hospitality Business	www.leisureandhospitalitybusiness.com	Leisure and hospitality

Newspaper	Web address	Primary market
Leisure Week	www.leisureweek.co.uk	Hospitality
London Careers	www.londoncareers.net	Admin/sec
Management Consultancy	www.managementconsultancy.vnu.co.uk	Management consultancy
Marketing Moves	www.marketing.haynet.com	Marketing
Marketing Week	www.mad.co.uk/mw	Marketing
Motor Trader	www.motortrader.com	Automotive
Nature	www.nature.com	Scientific
New Media Age	www.nma.co.uk	Media
New Scientist	www.newscientistjobs.com	Scientific
Nursing Standard	www.nursing-standard.co.uk	Nursing
Online Recruitment	www.onrec.com	Online recruitment
People Management	www.peoplemanagement.co.uk	Admin/sec
Personnel Today	www.personneltoday.com	Personnel
Post Magazine	www.postmag.co.uk	Insurance
PR Weekly	www.prweek.com	PR
Professional Recruiter	www.professional-recruiter.co.uk	Recruitment
Public Finance	www.publicfinance.co.uk	Public finance
Recruit Magazine	www.recruit.magazine.com	Recruitment
Revolution Magazine	www.uk.revolutionmagazine.com	New media
Science's Next Wave	www.nextwave.sciencemag.org	Scientific
Supply Management	www.supplymanagement.co.uk	Supply management
The Architectural Review	www.arplus.com	Architectural
The Caterer	www.caterer.com	Hospitality
The Economist	www.economist.com	Various
The Grocer	www.grocerjobs.co.uk	Sales and marketing
The Lancet	www.thelancet.com	Healthcare
The Law Gazette	www.lawgazette.co.uk	Legal
The Lawyer	www.the-lawyer.co.uk	Legal
The Stage	www.thestage.co.uk	Entertainment
Teaching Today	www.teaching-today.com	Education

7 Where else to look?

Job centres

The job centre is often overlooked by job hunters who are currently working and may be seen as the place which only the low-paid would visit in their search for jobs. Times have changed and if you have not visited a job centre for a while I have no doubt that you will be surprised by the wealth of information and help available to the job hunter.

The advent of technology has brought the job centre resource into the 21st century and most sites now have access to Jobpoint as well as online access via **www.jobcentreplus.gov.uk**. Jobpoints are user-friendly, touch screens that you can use to find information on vacancies held on the job bank both in the UK and throughout the EU.

Many employers and agencies will advertise their vacancies with the job centre prior to posting on the internet or spending money on a newspaper or trade publication advertisement, due to their ease of use and ability to tap into the local marketplace.

Job fairs

Job fairs are becoming an increasingly popular and cost-effective method of recruitment. The employer benefits from the opportunity to tap into a specific market area, for example IT graduates, as well as the chance to screen many potential employees over a short period of time. The job hunter benefits from the opportunity to meet with many different employers face to face and gain what could be termed a 'free' interview.

Getting prepared

Employers will size up candidates very quickly in a job fair environment so it is essential that you are prepared, prior to attending, to ensure that your time is well spent and productive:

- Obtain a list of participating employers from the sponsor of the job fair and identify any companies that interest you. Research these companies and prepare your knowledge in the same way you would for a 'real' interview scenario.

- Review your CV and ensure that you have at least 30 new copies to distribute at the job fair. Do not fold or staple your CV and ensure that it is targeted towards the type of employment you are seeking.

- Prepare yourself – always attend a job fair dressed as you would for a 'real' interview.

- Prepare your questions – think of some questions you will ask each individual employer based on the research you have conducted so far. Just imagine how much more effective and memorable you will be compared to the normal 'so what do you do?' type question that plagues employers at job fairs.

Dos and don'ts

Do take some time out to have a walk around the room when you first arrive to familiarise yourself with the layout and the locations of the employers you want to make contact with.

Do use your time in the line/queue to prepare your knowledge on the company further. You will have the edge over your fellow job hunters, as they will probably be staring into space waiting for their turn!

Do treat any form of contact with the employer as if you were in a 'real' interview, right down to eye contact and fluent communication. You may only have up to five minutes to make the right impression.

Do ask for a business card and write a follow-up letter.

Don't stand in line waiting to speak to an employer straightaway. If there is a line or queue at one of your targeted employers then approach them from the side and take a look through some of the literature available on their display. This will give you the opportunity to listen discreetly to the exchange of communication between the employer and the candidate they are currently interviewing/speaking to. Listen to what the employer is saying and be prepared to answer those types of questions. What would you say? Who are they currently recruiting? Does it sound interesting to you?

Career counsellors

There are a number of career/outplacement organisations operating across the UK marketplace. Career counselling helps people of all ages to make appropriate and realistic career choices. The range of services they provide are normally targeted towards individual senior managers looking for a change of career or large-scale contracts with companies making redundancies.

Career counselling assistance can include:

- identifying and matching job hunters' goals to interests and abilities
- looking at the range of jobs available in a chosen area of interest
- researching training or study available in a chosen area of interest
- planning a strategy to find available work in a chosen area of interest.

The main factor for job hunters to note is that most career counselling organisations are commercial companies and as such you can expect to pay for their services, which can be expensive, so bear this in mind when enlisting their services.

Networking

Did you know that networking through friends and contacts fills more than 26% of vacancies in the UK?

As soon as you start out on your job-hunting experience, the very act of telling family and friends that you are looking for a new/first job is the signal that you have commenced 'networking'.

Networking is vital for anyone considering a job change. Many people don't realise how important networking can be in their job search as the more contacts you make, the more opportunities you will hear about.

How do you network effectively?

Stay in touch with people

Don't be shy about getting in touch – give them a call or a quick email to let them know you are in the job market. Most people like to help, even if they can't offer you any immediate leads. The very act of planting the idea in their mind will ensure that if they hear about a suitable position they will think of you.

Tell everyone you know that you are searching for a job. Tell your friends and family and their friends. They may know of a job opportunity but won't let you know about it unless they know you are available.

Contact people you worked with in previous jobs. Don't let your business connections become a thing of the past – they can be your key to new employment opportunities.

Contact people you have made contact with in previous jobs, perhaps suppliers or customers depending on how friendly your relationship was with them. Let them know you are looking – they might just have an opportunity in the company they currently work in.

Develop new contacts

Always try to develop new employment contacts, perhaps through a club you are a member of or by joining a local society. If you are not currently working you could try voluntary work that will give you the added advantage of looking good on your CV. Any employer will be impressed with a CV that includes volunteer experience. Through relationships like this, you can make valuable contacts which you may otherwise not have had access to.

The more aggressive you are in your networking efforts, the more likely you are to benefit from this tried and tested method.

applying
for
the job

'There are no shortcuts to any place worth going.'

Anon

8 Application forms

Why do employers use them?

If you have prepared a good CV then you should have no trouble applying the same principles to an application form. Application forms are tailored in response to employers' specific requirements with the overall aim of easily identifying relevant information and suitable candidates. Employers want to be able to extract the same information from an application form as they would from a good CV, namely:

- skills
- achievements
- relevance.

As many as 95% of CVs received by employers in response to a vacancy advertisement will contain irrelevant information – imagine how long it would take to screen 100 of these CVs searching for the information that is important? For this reason many employers choose to use application forms to make the process of selecting candidates for interview a more structured and focused exercise, allowing every candidate to be screened on the same level and in direct comparison with each other. Application forms will also allow the employer to ask for information not normally included on a CV, as well as attracting only candidates who are seriously interested in the job due to the time taken to complete a good application.

While the application form process is designed to make candidate selection easier for employers it is not so user friendly towards potential employees. It requires time and effort to complete an application form to the best of your ability and the process is as demanding each and every time you complete one.

Before you start completing the form take the time to read through carefully and follow any instructions, for example:

- Use black ink and complete in block capitals.
- Take a photocopy of the original to use as your draft copy.
- Ensure you have a copy of the original job advertisement, your CV and any additional information available on the organisation such as website information, company brochure etc.
- Answer every question. If the question does not apply to you then write 'Not applicable' across the box or section to highlight to the employer that you have not accidentally omitted answering the question.

Let's take a look at a sample application form and discuss the key sections.

Glasgow City Council
PLEASE COMPLETE ALL DETAILS IN BLOCK CAPITALS USING BLACK INK

SECTION 1 – DETAILS OF VACANCY

Job title _____   Department _____

Reference number	Closing date
From what source did you learn of this vacancy? If job centre, please state which:	Please give details of any dates during next six weeks when you would not be available for interview

SECTION 2 – PERSONAL DETAILS

Surname _____ Forename(s) _____

Address _____

_____

Postcode

Home tel _____ Mobile _____ Work tel _____

Driving licence   Yes/No

Leisure interests

_____

_____

_____

_____

_____

_____

_____

_____

_____

_____

SECTION 3 – EQUAL OPPORTUNITIES

The following information is required in order that equal opportunity policies can be monitored effectively. The aim of the policy is to ensure that no job applicant receives less favourable treatment on the grounds of race, disability, sex or age.

Date of birth _____ Age _____ Sex _____ Male/Female_____

Are you disabled? _____ Are you registered? _____

If you answered Yes above, please give brief details _____

_____

_____

Please describe your racial or ethnic origin UK/European _____ Indian _____

Pakistan _____ African/Caribbean _____

Other (please specify) _____

SECTION 4 – EDUCATION DETAILS

Dates (from/to)	School/College/University	Qualifications gained	Grade

SECTION 5 – TRAINING COURSES

Attendance at training courses relevant to your employment

Organising body	Course title	Duration	Date

SECTION 6 – MEMBERSHIP OF PROFESSIONAL BODIES

Body	Grade of membership	Whether by exam	Date

SECTION 7 – EMPLOYMENT HISTORY

(starting with most recent)

Dates (from/to)	Employer's name and address	Job title and brief description of duties

Salary on leaving £ _____ Notice period _____

Reason for leaving _____

Previous employment

Dates (from/to)	Employer's name and address	Job title and brief description of duties

Salary on leaving £ _____ Notice period _____

Reason for leaving _____

Dates (from/to)	Employer's name and address	Job title and brief description of duties

Salary on leaving £ _____ Notice period_____

Reason for leaving _____

SECTION 8 – RELEVANT INFORMATION

Other relevant information and experience

The information you provide in this section is important in assessing your application. Please use this space to state your reasons for applying for the post, relating your skills, experience and personal qualities to the requirements of the job. You may include relevant details of the following: gaps in paid employment, unpaid work experience, voluntary activities, leisure interests and positions of responsibility held.

If you require more space please attach a separate sheet.

SECTION 9 – REFERENCES

Give the names of two persons to whom reference may be made in respect of your application. The first should be your last employer (or head teacher if school leaver). Referees are only contacted if candidates are to be interviewed, but if you do not wish a referee to be contacted until after a provisional offer of employment is made, please indicate in the appropriate box.

Reference 1 – present employer
Name
Address
Position
Telephone number
Contact prior to offer   Yes/No (please circle)

Reference 2 – previous employer
Name
Address
Position
Telephone number
Contact prior to offer   Yes/No (please circle)

SECTION 10 – DECLARATION

I declare that the information given in this application is true and that I have not withheld any information that might reasonably affect my suitability for employment with Glasgow City Council.

Signed _____   Date _____

Key sections

Details of vacancy

Almost every application form will contain details of the vacancy somewhere near to the beginning of the form. Local government, hospitals, civil service positions will usually use application forms in their recruitment process. They are likely to conduct ongoing recruitment over a wide variety of departments and for this reason it is important for the primary recruiter (usually an HR professional) to ascertain quickly and easily exactly which post you are applying for. If you are unsure exactly what to include relate back to the original job advertisement, which should contain the details you are seeking.

Personal details

The personal details section normally contains exactly the same information you would expect to find in a CV: your name, your address and how to contact you.

If asked driving questions in this section state your current situation; if, for example, you are currently learning to drive or have a test date booked then say so, if you are asked if you have a clean licence, be honest or it may come back to haunt you later.

Equal opportunities

Many employers monitor their recruitment and selection process to ensure that they are operating a fair equal opportunities programme. The information supplied in this section will not be used as part of the selection process and is designed to protect you against discrimination.

Education details

Unless specifically asked for, only supply details that relate to your education from secondary school onwards.

Training courses

This section is a good way to make you stand out from your contemporaries during the application process. If you have been fortunate enough to undertake training courses with your present and previous employers then include them in this section.

Membership of professional bodies

This section is designed for professional membership bodies relating to your employment history, e.g. IPD, ACCA, SIMA etc.

Employment history

The employment history section, as in a CV, is designed to indicate to an employer whether you *can do* the job. Before completing this section take some time out to read the job advertisement again and relate your experience to the job description. As you would in the preparation of a CV remember to highlight the experience that is relevant to the post you are applying for. Use recognisable job titles and ensure that your dates follow in a chronological manner; be sure to look out for any gaps in your employment history and include them in the form, e.g. May 82 – August 90: career break to look after children.

Salary on leaving

While I do not recommend including your salary details in a CV there is little you can do to avoid the question when included in an application form. If you choose to omit the information it will be very apparent to an employer and it could be the difference between getting an interview or not.

Reason for leaving

No matter what your reason for leaving a previous position always try to reflect your decision-making process in a positive manner. You could for example have left a previous organisation because you 'felt under-appreciated', but rather than include this as the reason it would read so much better if you stated your reasons as something like 'to obtain better prospects with more responsibility'. Always be aware that what you put down on paper can be misunderstood by the reader, so be sure to state clearly and positively your reasons in a way that can plainly only have one meaning.

Relevant information

This section is the most important part of the application form. It is where you get the opportunity to highlight your skills and achievements to an employer and make them relevant to the position you are applying for, as well as personalising the section to you. In the same way you use your CV as a sales brochure to highlight your abilities, this whole section is your opportunity to sell your skills and achievements to an employer.

Before completing this section take a blank piece of paper and draw a line down the middle. On the left-hand side write down everything you know about the job requirements and on the right-hand side match up where your skills and achievements bear relevance.

Personnel secretary – Glasgow City Council

Job requirements	My skills and achievements
1 Fully conversant with MS Office packages	1 Fully conversant with MS Office packages – over five years' experience
2 Ability to work as part of a team	2 Currently working as part of a small team
3 Previous supervisory experience	3 Supervising four support secretaries – six years' experience in a supervisory role

Reasons for applying

Always the most difficult question! What are your reasons for looking for another job? Perhaps you want more responsibility and feel that this position could offer you the career progression that you are seeking. In that case you could open your narrative with the statement:

Having worked in a secretarial role for the past six years I am now seeking a position that can offer me career progression to the next level within a large organisation. I feel that the position of Senior Secretary within the Planning Department of Glasgow City Council offers the key characteristics I seek, namely (a) career progression, (b) more responsibility and (c) the ability to work closely within a small team.

Examine your reasons for wanting to leave your current position as they will provide the pointers as to why you feel this position is right for you.

This section is also the area where you get the opportunity to include areas of experience that are relevant to the position you are applying for, that have been gained outside the paid employment arena. Remember back to our discussion of Sally's worksheets where we identified that she could use her experience leading the Brownie pack in future job applications. If you haven't read that section then take a look at it now; it may help you in completing this section and ensure that you proceed to the interview stage.

It is likely that you will rewrite this section several times on a draft piece of paper before you are happy with the final result. Aim to fill at least three-quarters of the page and ensure that your handwriting is clear and legible, use a ruler to assist you in following a straight line if you feel you have the tendency to slant off in a particular direction. Check your spelling or even better ask a family member to check it for you. When you are happy that everything is in order transfer the information from the draft application form to the original.

Do not include your CV with the finished application form to be sent off to the employer unless you are specifically asked to do so. If you feel you need more space to sell your abilities then attach a separate sheet of paper on to this section, clearly marking at the top of the page your name, address, telephone number and position applied for.

Include a covering letter with your application form (some examples follow in the next chapter).

Keep a copy of the application form to help you prepare for interview and post the original off to the employer in an A4 envelope at least three days prior to the closing date. If you are unsure whether the application will arrive in time then consider delivering by hand or using a guaranteed next-day delivery service.

9 Covering letters

Do I need to send a covering letter?

When you send an application form or a CV you should always accompany it with a covering letter. The covering letter should be afforded the same amount of effort as a CV/application form as it will give the employer their first impression of you. It could make the difference between your CV/application form being given a casual glance or encouraging the employer to read on.

Think of your covering letter as a 'sales pitch' to sell your abilities to a potential employer, it is your opportunity to state to the employer why they should read your CV/application form with care and invite you forward to the next stage – the interview.

If you haven't applied for a job in a long time, the thought of writing a letter may seem a little daunting. As a general rule most business letters in the UK today follow the same layout pattern. I have included some samples for you to use as a guide and hopefully you can see that the language used is very similar to other letters you may have written in the past as part of your daily life.

The main difference between a job-hunting letter and any other type of letter you write is the subject matter contained within the main body – employers are interested in finding out what you can do for them as opposed to what they can do for you. In an earlier section when we discussed the importance of using power words in your CV to highlight your skills and achievements, the same principle should be applied to your covering letter. Your covering letter is a powerful tool in your job-hunting search that should be used to highlight your unique selling points – the things that make you different from everyone else out there.

There are three main types of covering letter to consider when job hunting:

- covering letter to accompany CV/application form in response to an advertisement
- cold/speculative letter
- networking letter.

Covering letter to accompany CV/application form in response to an advertisement

A covering letter in response to an advertised vacancy is probably the easiest of the three to put down on paper. Your reader will be expecting to receive it and will already have provided you with clues as to the identity of the ideal candidate they are seeking. For you, the job hunter, it is simply a matter of identifying these clues and applying them to your CV/application form and covering letter.

Cold/speculative letter

The cold/speculative letter takes an entirely different tack by attempting to communicate with the reader without having a clear idea of their needs and wants. The important thing to remember when using this job-hunting tool is to research your market and apply the principle of quality and not quantity. Cold/speculative letters have been proved to work if you target your market correctly, making it more likely that your reader will have a real interest and, more importantly, a need for your skills and abilities. Sending a generic letter to lots of employers in the hope of getting a job offer just won't work.

Networking letter

The networking letter differs from the previous two in that you are merely making contact with the reader on the recommendation of another. You are, in effect, setting out your unique selling points in the hope that the reader may be to able assist you. Always state in the letter how you got the reader's name and say why you are writing. Often letters like this will lead to openings within the hidden job market, discussed in a later section of the book.

Each of these types of letter will take on a slightly different form, although they will all broadly speaking cover three main paragraphs.

Paragraph one

Used to convey your reason for writing; attempt to grasp the employer's attention straight away, for example:

- Your advertisement in the *London Evening Standard* on 25 October was of great interest . . .

- As a major competitor of Brown's Engineering Tools I have followed your recent results very closely . . .

- Your recent article in *IT Weekly* . . .

- Your excellent reputation within the engineering community . . .

- I read with interest an article in the *Glasgow Evening Times* that you are opening a new store in . . .

Paragraph two

Where you get the chance to sell your skills and abilities to the employer, customise this paragraph to highlight where your qualities can make a difference. Pay particular attention to the job advertisement (if applicable) and highlight the key areas that the employer is looking for. Imagine the sales brochure – it needs to be relatively short and straight to the point, don't be tempted to repeat too much information verbatim from your CV, pick out two or three key points that you feel would be of interest to the employer and, more importantly, encourage them to read your CV/application form in detail:

- The prime focus of my career within business development has included 5 years as Sales Director at Brown and Smith Engineering. I have been responsible for the development of various successful sales strategies on an international level . . .

- Customer services has been the main focus of my career during the past ten years, including six years at a supervisory level . . .

- As an experienced and highly motivated sales assistant with ten years' experience within a textile sales environment . . .

- Seven years Windows NT experience as a stand-alone platform, together with fluency in French and German . . .

Paragraph three

This final paragraph is where you tie up the letter and request to be taken forward to the next stage:

- I look forward to the opportunity of discussing the vacancy in more detail.

- I would welcome the chance to meet with you and discuss the position.

- I am particularly interested in this position and would value the opportunity to meet and discuss this application in more detail.

- I would value the opportunity to discuss any suitable positions in more detail.

- I believe that I would have a great deal to offer Brown and Smith Engineering and am keen to be considered for any appropriate opportunities.

Dos and don'ts of covering letters

Do use good quality A4 white paper.

Do use the same font/typeface as your CV.

Do check spelling and ask someone else to double check.

Do write to a named contact.

Do keep the letter to one side of an A4 page.

Do customise every covering letter.

Do be relevant in paragraph two but don't attempt to copy verbatim from your CV.

Do use business English, e.g. Dear Ms Evans . . . Yours sincerely.

Do use clear and official language.

Don't be tempted to write in an overly familiar manner.

Don't handwrite your covering letter unless specifically asked to do so.

Don't project an overly arrogant or obnoxious tone.

Finally, your covering letter is the packaging for your CV and more importantly *you* – does it represent your skills and achievements adequately and encourage the employer to invite you forward for interview?

Sample covering letters

Standard letter layout

Your address
and telephone number
(If you do not have a
telephone then ask a
friend or relative
if you may use theirs.)

Today's date

Name, job title and address of the person you are writing to

Dear . . .

(Try to avoid the use of Dear Sir/Madam in your job applications. If you do not know the name of the intended individual why not ring the company to find out. The name should be transferred to the letter in the form Ms Jones or Mr Smith – never use first names.)

Title and reference number of the job you are applying for

Main body of letter

Yours . . .
(Sincerely if Dear Mr/Ms
Faithfully if Dear Sir/Madam)
Your signature
(Print your name below.)
Enc (at the end of the letter to signify an enclosure)

Covering letter to accompany cv in response to advertised vacancy

25 Newberry Gardens
Newton Mearns
Glasgow G78 1PG

12 July 2002

Mr Stephen Jones
Sales Director
Jones and Sons Engineering
45 Sunny Street
Glasgow G89 2PL

Dear Mr Brown

Re: Business development manager – *The Herald*, 11 July 2002

Your advertisement in *The Herald* on 11 July 2002 was of great interest to me and I believe that my skills and previous experience would make a real contribution to the future plans of your organisation.

The prime focus of my career within business development has included five years as sales manager at Brown and Smith Engineering. I have been responsible for the development of various successful sales strategies on an international level and, heading a team of six, was responsible for achieving at least 250% of budget over the past two consecutive years.

I am particularly interested in this position and would value the opportunity to meet and discuss this application in more detail.

Yours sincerely

John Smith

Enc

Cold/speculative letter

25 Newberry Gardens
Newton Mearns
Glasgow G78 1PG

12 July 2002

Mr Stephen Jones
Area Manager
Asda Superstores
45 Sunny Street
Glasgow G89 2PL

Dear Mr Jones

I read with interest an article in the *Glasgow Evening Times* on 11 July 2002 that you are to open a new store in Bishopbriggs in November 2002.

As an experienced and highly motivated sales assistant with ten years' experience within a retail environment I would be particularly interested in finding out more about your opportunities. As you will see from my CV I have an excellent work record and have achieved consistently throughout my career.

I would value the opportunity to discuss any suitable positions in more detail and look forward to hearing from you.

Yours sincerely

Margaret Phillips

Enc

Networking letter

25 Newberry Gardens
Newton Mearns
Glasgow G78 1PG

12 July 2002

Mr Stephen Jones
Managing Director
Steel and Timber Merchants
45 Sunny Street
Glasgow G89 2PL

Dear Mr Jones

I have followed your company's progress with interest over the last few years, especially in my capacity as sales director of one of your main competitors Browns Steel and Timber. We have been especially strong in the East European marketplace and I noticed that you have recently entered that area of operations.

I spoke with a good friend of mine recently, Stuart Smith, MD of Smith Steel Fabrications, who suggested that I write to you.

My extensive experience of business development within the East European market has been developed over the past five years and as you have recently entered the arena I would like to offer my experience and proven abilities to help develop your organisation into the market leader.

I would be delighted to discuss any opportunities you may have available and I enclose a copy of my CV for your perusal. Perhaps I could telephone you next week to arrange a suitable time to meet?

Yours sincerely

Alan Jennings

Enc

10 Telephone interviews

Why a telephone interview?

Telephone interviews are becoming increasingly popular as a method of pre-screening applicants prior to face-to-face interviewing. Employers may decide to embark on this method in response to applications for a specific job as well as following up speculative applications by potential candidates.

Many employers favour this approach to streamline their recruitment processes making the whole process a much leaner and less time-consuming machine. Employers benefit from the ability to interview candidates from a much wider geographical location in much greater numbers than they would at a face-to-face interview. A pile of CVs in response to a job ad can very quickly be cut down to a manageable number of shortlisted candidates.

For you, the job hunter, the telephone interview has a number of advantages and disadvantages over its face-to-face counterpart. Telephone interviews give you unlimited control over the setting and environment of the interview. On the other hand, it does not allow you to see or respond to the non-verbal clues available in abundance at a face-to-face interview.

The goal of a telephone interview from an employer's point of view is to eliminate unsuitable candidates and come up with a shortlist to invite forward to the next stage. As a job hunter your goal is to ensure that you have made adequate preparation for the telephone interview in order to proceed forward to that next stage.

Getting organised for a telephone interview

Getting organised for a telephone interview, whether of the expected or unexpected variety, will help you to feel mentally prepared for the moment the interviewer rings your number. Before you start, let's look at a few key areas of preparation:

- If you have an answering machine, check the message. Is it professional? Does it portray the impression you want to give to an employer? If not, change it!

- Remove call waiting from your telephone as it could be distracting to both you and the interviewer.

- Keep details of all the jobs you have applied for together with your research data on each in separate folders close to the telephone. These will be especially important in the case of unexpected telephone interviews where your ability quickly and easily to slip into the persona of a prepared candidate will afford you an advantage over your fellow job hunters.

- Inform your family or anyone else who lives with you within reach of the telephone that you may receive a call from a prospective employer. If you have young children at home who have developed a passion for running to answer the telephone first, try to move it out of their way for the time being!

- Your verbal communication skills are vital at this stage of the interview process; how you sound to the interviewer will form a large part of the selection procedure. As strange as it may seem your body language is every bit as important during a telephone interview as it is during a face-to-face one. The interviewer cannot see you but they will start to form an impression of you based on the way you sound, in other words the sound of your voice is as much a selling tool as the things you say. Your voice should be pleasant and enthusiastic, practise smiling on the phone – it will automatically give your voice a lift and make a major difference to how you sound to the interviewer. Try it with your family and friends to see if they can notice the difference. Standing up while on the telephone is a trick used by many professionals. It will make you feel more confident and in control and give you the added advantage of projecting your voice. Use a tape recorder or family and friends to practise some interview questions and answers with. How do you sound? The aim should be to sound like an individual with an enthusiastic, relaxed and confident approach who maintains the interviewer's interest throughout the conversation.

- Prepare an interview pack to keep by the telephone; it should contain your CV, pen/pencil and a pad of paper to write on.

- Prepare for a telephone interview in the same way you would for a face-to-face interview. Because the interviewer cannot see you, the things that you say will be their only clue to your suitability. Read Chapter 14 on interviews to help you to be fully prepared and to provide you with guidance on the preparation you should undertake prior to communicating directly with the employer.

■ Allow anywhere between 15 and 30 minutes for the interview.

■ Avoid distractions at all costs – if you are waiting on a prescheduled telephone interview then ensure your telephone is in a quiet part of the house, turn off the TV and if you have children or a dog persuade them to move to another part of the house. If you receive a call unexpectedly it is OK to take a few moments to compose yourself and take the actions outlined to avoid distractions. If this is not possible then ask the interviewer if you can rearrange a more suitable time for you to call back. Although this takes away the spontaneity that employers sometimes enjoy it is better to be prepared and give a good account of yourself than not.

During the telephone interview

When the telephone rings right about the time of your interview it perfectly natural to feel slightly apprehensive, so take a few moments to compose yourself, pick up the receiver and speak slowly and clearly. As long as you have done your preparation for this interview there is nothing to worry about. Just concentrate on projecting your voice in an enthusiastic and confident manner while referring to your CV and research material.

■ As introductions are made, jot down the name of the interviewer(s) to enable you to refer to them by name as required.

■ Roughly jot down a tough question while repeating it out loud to the interviewer. This will give you time to think and ensure that you remain relevant in your answer. Because you and the interviewer are relying solely on verbal communication you cannot pick up on valuable non-verbal clues and it is therefore wise when dealing with a particularly difficult or detailed question to ask the interviewer if you have provided enough detail in your answer or if they require more information in a specific area.

■ Remember, short sentences are more powerful than long rambling narrations. Short sentences keep the interest up between both parties and allow for interchange between you and the interviewer(s).

■ If you are unclear about a question, ask the interviewer to repeat it. Expect minor miscommunication, especially when there is more than one interviewer.

■ Ask a few well thought-out questions at the end of the interview (refer to Chapter 15 for guidance) and afford the interviewer(s) the normal courtesy of thanking them for their time.

Dos and don'ts of telephone interviews

Do prepare both yourself and your knowledge as you would for a face-to-face interview.

Do relax and enjoy the experience. The more you practise the better you will become.

Don't be afraid of silences and be tempted to keep talking long after your point has been made

Don't be overly familiar with the interviewer because you are in your own environment, stick to the normal interview etiquette as if you were sitting in front of them.

Don't smoke or drink during an interview; telephones are famed for their ability to amplify noise.

Don't use too many umms and ahhs – they are more noticeable during a telephone interview.

Don't let frustration or disappointment creep into your voice; these emotions are picked up much more easily over the telephone than face to face.

11 Assessment centres

Why do employers use assessment centres?

Assessment centres have gained in popularity in recent years and many companies now see them as an important part of their selection process. The advantage of assessment centres over any other type of recruitment process is that they allow employers to see multiple potential employees whom they can directly compare using a series of tasks in a single session.

What can I expect?

Assessment centres normally involve a group of candidates (typically between 6 and 12) who are assessed over a period of time, lasting anywhere between a few hours to a few days, on a variety of different tasks. Assessment centres vary depending on the role and the organisation, but here are some of the typical processes you can expect.

Group discussions or specified tasks

These types of assessment are designed to test how well you work and integrate with others. Typically, the group will be set a task or topic of discussion and given a timeframe to work to. The employer may select a task that would have a direct relevance on the position you are applying for, but it is equally likely that they pick something completely off the wall, so do try to be prepared for anything. Discussions will often be focused towards a topical item of news – be careful of getting embroiled in a political or discriminatory discussion as you could reveal opinions that you would keep to yourself in other circumstances.

Many people jump headfirst into the task and discussion scenarios by taking charge and directing the others in the group in an attempt to highlight their leadership abilities to the observers. If you are this type of personality beware you do not become overpowering and affect the balance of the group. At the opposite end of the scale if you are quiet and perhaps feeling overpowered by stronger personalities then ensure that you contribute to the group discussions, even if only to show that you have an opinion either way.

Presentations

These types of task are normally directed at a group and intended to ascertain how well you integrate with others as well as your ability to clarify and present information. The group will normally be given a subject for presentation and assigned preparation time appropriate to the task at hand. Typically, when strangers are put together in this type of scenario several potential leaders will emerge from the group fairly quickly, each with an opinion on how the presentation should be constructed, often wasting valuable time on a battle of egos! Remember – the assessors are attempting to identify key characteristics when observing group presentations, not who has the best idea. Stand out by considering and discussing your fellow interviewees' points of view, contributing your own ideas and ensuring that the discussion remains relevant and focused.

Roleplays

The dreaded roleplay usually makes an appearance at most group assessments and interviews up and down the country. Roleplays are often used to recreate a particular aspect of the role you are applying for, for example, it could be an angry customer or problem member of staff. Whatever the case, the employer is attempting to assess how you would react if faced with the real thing. Many people are uncomfortable with roleplays, but the secret is to just enjoy the situation and try to behave in your normal manner.

Psychometric assessments

Employers will often choose to introduce psychometric testing during some part of the interview process and many favour it at assessment centres. (Refer to Chapter 13 for more information on the types of assessment you may face.)

Interviews

Largely depending on the requirements of the role, employers will normally conduct either 1:1 or panel interviews with candidates attending assessment centres.

Dos and don'ts of assessment centre interviews

Do try to be yourself, no matter what is thrown in your way. It is as important for you to feel that you fit in with the company and its culture, as it is for the company to choose the right individual for the role.

Do remain polite and friendly towards other candidates, no matter how they are behaving.

Do try to contribute visibly towards any group discussions or tasks – show the observers your ability to interact and consider others' points of view.

Do watch out if you are involved in an assessment that requires you to remain overnight and watch your alcohol intake in the evening – you will be observed for the duration of the assessment period, not just the classroom exercises.

Don't attempt to control or manipulate the group.

Don't scorn others' opinions no matter what you really think of them.

Don't allow yourself to become disheartened if there are others in the group who seem to be taking control – that may not be what the employer is looking for.

12 Panel interviews

What are panel interviews?

Panel interviews can strike fear into the most confident of job hunters, but the good news is that they can actually work to your advantage. Typically, a panel interview will consist of around two to six people drawn from a range of positions within the organisation and usually includes:

■ one person with a detailed working knowledge of the requirements of the position, normally a supervisor

■ one person trained in selection techniques, normally an HR professional

■ One person from the executive or general staff.

Panel interviewing tends to be less subjective than 1:1 interviewing, as you have a greater chance of making a positive and lasting impression with at least one member of the panel, who could prove to be your leverage tool to proceed on to the next stage.

Having to face more than one interviewer can be more intimidating and stressful because it poses greater challenges than the traditional 1:1 interview. You will have to be extra alert and focused since you are likely to be faced with questions thrown one after the other from different interviewers, giving you less time to think and formulate answers.

The key to a successful panel interview is to ensure that you have prepared thoroughly for it. Adequate preparation will arm you with enough information about yourself and the company to create the right impression and give you the confidence you need to stand out above your fellow interviewees. Remember, the interviewers want you to do well – now it's up to you!

Format of a panel interview

■ Most interviews will follow a similar format, depending on the selection panel. Expect the interview to last between 30 and 45 minutes.

■ Panel members will usually take it in turns to ask you pre-prepared questions that they will present to all candidates being interviewed for the position.

■ One member of the panel will generally chair the interview.

■ Normally, the panel will ask you questions first and invite you to ask questions at the end of the interview.

■ It is usual for panel members to take notes throughout the interview to assist them with the decision-making process. Don't allow their scribbling to put you off.

Top tips on panel interviews

■ When you enter the room make eye contact with each of the interviewers and remember to smile and relax.

■ If possible, write down the names of the interviewers together with their job function allowing you to direct your answers towards their particular area of expertise, as well as using their names in your answers. Take care not to be over-familiar with the use of first names.

■ Make eye contact with the person who asks you a question and as you continue move your eyes along the panel to make eye contact with the next person and so on. Finish your answer back with the person who originated the question. This method will ensure that you address all members of the panel and keep their interest and focus on your answer.

■ Try to establish the leader of the group and make a special effort to impress that person.

■ Attempt to establish rapport with the group by identifying the various personality types within the panel, find ways to connect with each of them.

■ Remember to smile and convey enthusiasm at all times during the interview.

■ Ask questions to give yourself some thinking time and breathing space.

13 Psychometric testing

Another composite word, this time: *psycho* meaning mind and *metric* meaning measure.

Why do employers use psychometric testing?

As employers seek to control staffing turnover levels and recruitment budgets they are increasingly looking for additional tools to assist them in the cost-effective selection of new recruits. In order to be prepared for any eventuality you need to be aware of the tools employers use in order to understand and prepare for them. In the course of this chapter we will look at:

- ability testing
- aptitude testing
- personality testing.

Many employers believe that psychometric testing will give them an accurate prediction of an individual's suitability for a particular role and research has shown that this method is far more reliable than a normal standalone interview.

Employers can choose to introduce psychometric testing at any stage of the selection process. Some use them at the very beginning to screen out unsuitable candidates while others use the more favoured approach of using them as a tool after the first or second interview. These tests if used properly are designed only to assist the employer in making a decision about the candidate; they may provide them with some valuable information that can be further explored in a traditional interview setting. They should never be used as the sole method of assessing suitability and are not designed to do so. All reputable organisations offering psychometric tests in today's market govern their use with strict guidelines and they are most often only available for use under licence. This ensures that the tests can only be administered by competent assessors and provides guidelines as to the correct manner of administration.

While you cannot prepare for psychometric testing in the same manner as you would for a traditional examination where memory and recall are more often the guiding factors, you can familiarise yourself with the typical questions found in psychometric tests. There are numerous books and online sites offering the chance to practise psychometric tests and I would strongly recommend that you take the time to undertake some of these practice sessions to prepare yourself. It is normal in most psychometric assessments to be given the opportunity to try some practice questions prior to embarking on the real thing and these are invaluable as they should set your mind at ease and ensure that you understand the manner in which the questions operate. Remember that these assessments are not designed to catch you out, they are as valuable to you as an individual in identifying the right job for you as they are to an employer for identifying the right employee for them.

Ability testing

Ability testing measures an individual's potential for specific skills; it focuses on what a person is capable of achieving as opposed to what they may have achieved in the past. Obviously, some previous knowledge of the subject matter is required before ability can be tested; for example, if the employer wished to assess your numerical ability then you would require some previous knowledge of mathematics or arithmetic.

General ability is usually divided up into specific ability sectors designed to be scored and interpreted individually or together as part of a general ability measure. A general ability test could be composed of specific numerical, verbal and spatial scales to assist the employer in identifying your areas of strength and weakness.

Confused? Don't be, these tests are designed to assess your potential and as such should be viewed as an enjoyable experience to help you understand yourself better.

Let's take a look at a common ability test focusing on verbal reasoning skills. The tests normally consist of a short story accompanied by a number of short paragraphs that are used to convey information. You are then invited to say whether the information in the paragraph is true, false or impossible to say, for example:

- **True** – The statement has been made in the passage.
- **False** – The statement contradicts a statement made in the passage.
- **Impossible to say** – There is insufficient information in the passage to confirm either true or false.

Read through this passage and then look at the four statements that follow:

In winter, outdoor swimming pools are generally shut down, so you will only need to check on it sporadically and add a winter-care product until you reopen it for summer. If you would prefer, it is possible to hire someone from a pool dealer to take over the maintenance for you. In the summer, looking after the pool should only take about one hour every week and will involve checking the pH balance in the water and clearing debris from the skimmer baskets. Bacteria are killed off using sanitisers and the most common chemicals used for this are chlorine or bromide. The amount you will need will depend from day to day so use a test kit to check the level required.

Statement 1   In winter there is no need to look after the pool.

Statement 2   The pH level should be between 5.5 and 6.

Statement 3   Bacteria are killed off using sanitisers and bromide.

Statement 4   You should use a test kit to check on the levels of chemicals required.

Statement 1 is false. The passage stated that you should check on it sporadically and add a winter-care product.

Statement 2 is impossible to say. The passage stated that you should check the pH balance; it did not state what the balance should be, therefore it is impossible to say if between 5.5 and 6 is true or false.

Statement 3 is true. The passage stated that bacteria could be killed off using sanitisers and common chemicals including chlorine and bromide.

Statement 4 is true. The passage stated that a test kit should be used to check the levels.

How did you do? Most questions in verbal reasoning psychometric assessments are no more difficult than this example. You may be up against the clock in the real thing, but the secret is to remain calm and focus on what the question states and what conclusion you can draw from the information contained in the passage.

Let's take a look at a numerical ability test; these assessments are designed to assess your skill at reasoning with numbers. First, you are given some information that can be presented in a variety of forms, e.g. text, tables or graphs and followed by questions with four possible answers.

The employee bonus scheme is intended to reward the high achievers with an extra cash incentive paid on a monthly basis. The threshold for every employee is £6,000 revenue per month and bonus payments are staged into the following percentage ratios:

a   £0–£6,000 – 4% only payable if threshold achieved

b   £6,000–£8,000 – 8%

c   £8,000–£10,000 – 10%

d   £10,00–£15,000 – 15%

e   £15,000 + – 20%

Bonus is only paid out if the employee reaches the lower threshold.

This example was provided prior to the start of the assessment to ensure that candidates fully understood the methodology behind the question.

John achieved £13,000 of revenue in January and has accrued a bonus payment of:

   a   £2,000
   b   £1,465
   c   £1,600
   d   £1,050

The correct answer is **d £1050** calculated as follows:

£0–£6,000 = 4% of the first £6,000 = £240
£6,000–£8,000 = 8% of the next £2,000 = £160
£8,000–£10,000 = 10% of the next £2,000 = £200
£10,000–£13,000 = 15% of the final £3,000 = £450

Let's try another three questions to get your brain moving in the right direction.

Question 1 – How much commission was Steven due on £10,000 of revenue?

   a   £2,000
   b   Nil
   c   £600
   d   £800

Question 2 – How much commission was Carrie due on £5,800 of revenue?

   a £200

   b £500

   c Nil

   d £350

Question 3 – How much commission was Abby due on £16,000 of revenue?

   a £1,000

   b £12,000

   c Nil

   d £1,550

Question 1 – **c £600**, calculated as:

   £0–£6,000 = 4% × £6,000 = £240

   £6,000–£8,000 = 8% × £2,000 = £160

   £8,000–£10,000 = 10% × £2,000 = £200

Question 2 – **c Nil**, as employees do not qualify for commission on revenue of less than £6,000.

Question 3 – **d £1550**, calculated as:

   £0–£6,000 = 4% × £6,000 = £240

   £6,000–£8,000 = 8% × £2,000 = £160

   £8,000–£10,000 = 10% × £2,000 = £200

   £10,000–£15,000 = 15% × £5,000 = £70

   £15,000+ = 20% of the final £1,000 = £200

Aptitude testing

Aptitude testing and ability testing are almost identical; the main accepted difference is that aptitude is used to measure a specific ability whereas ability is used to measure your general ability. Organisations offering aptitude testing tend to focus them towards specific jobs, for example computer programming aptitude testing or mechanical aptitude testing. To you as the job hunter there will be no clear identifiable difference between aptitude and ability testing. To help with examples simply concentrate on the tests commonly found in ability testing.

Personality testing

As we have discussed earlier, it is important to both the job hunter and the employer that an individual *will fit* into an organisation. Your personality will, to a large extent, control the types of environment you will be most comfortable in and where you feel comfortable and accepted you are most likely to perform your job role to a higher standard. Personality is to a great extent already set in place; we can adjust certain facets to suit circumstances but will always revert back to type eventually. It is important when answering questions set that you attempt to be objective and answer as truthfully as possible, try not to answer as you think the employer would want you to. These tests normally have a number of built-in mechanisms designed to spot inconsistencies in your answers, so minimise any confusion or inconsistencies by following a pattern of objectivity.

As with other types of psychometric testing you will usually be provided with a number of examples prior to embarking on the actual personality test. As shown in the following example, you will normally be presented with a statement and asked to provide your response to it in one of a number of options, for example: No one would blame me for taking an extra long lunch after working particularly hard.

Strongly agree	Agree	Unsure	Disagree	Strongly disagree

In the test you would be asked to select one of these five options ranging from strongly agree to strongly disagree. It is often the case in these types of test that you consider more than more of the answers to be correct, however the whole point of the test is to allow you only one answer. Remember, answer according to your instinct and don't take too long to ponder all the eventualities.

In the next example, each of the rows contains four descriptive words. Place M in the box next to the word that most describes your behaviour and L in the box next to the word that least describes your behaviour. Each row should then contain one M, one L and two open spaces.

Remember:

■ The analysis is not a test. There are no 'right' or 'wrong' answers.

■ The profile must be completed in isolation and without interruption.

- Try to be as spontaneous as possible.
- When completing the profile, think of yourself in your current job (as opposed to your home or social environment).

The individual given in the example perceives him or herself as most original and least gentle of the four words in the first row.

GENTLE	L	PERSUASIVE		HUMBLE		ORIGINAL	M
Gentle		Persuasive		Humble		Original	
Attractive		Dutiful		Stubborn		Pleasant	
Easily led		Bold		Loyal		Charming	
Open minded		Obliging		Will power		Cheerful	
Jovial		Precise		Courageous		Even tempered	
Competitive		Considerate		Happy		Harmonious	
Fussy		Obedient		Unconquerable		Playful	
Brave		Inspiring		Submissive		Timid	

(*Source*: Adapted from Thomas International Limited PPA.
For further information on Thomas International see www.careeradvisor.co.uk)

14 The interview

A job interview is probably one of the few situations in life in which even the most confident among us can suffer from cold feet. As soon as we receive confirmation that our great CV/application form has been selected to move on to the interview stage, we start to remind ourselves of all the reasons why we won't get the job. We recall past interviews that did not turn out as expected or other equally negative scenarios and almost immediately start to put doubts in our minds about the chances of success. If you recognise yourself as one of these individuals bear the following important points in mind:

- You have been selected for interview based on the skills and experience contained within your CV/application form.

- You will only be selected for an interview if the employer thinks you can do the job.

- You will likely be one of around five or six being interviewed, prior preparation can help you produce an outstanding performance and proceed to the next stage.

Be confident about your own abilities. You have arrived at the interview stage due to the time and effort you have put into the job-hunting process so far.

What is the employer looking for?

Earlier in the book we discussed the amount of effort the employer will put into the process of finding the right candidate for their job. They may already have contributed a great deal of time and money to proceed to the stage when they are ready to interview candidates whom they consider have the right amount of skills and experience to do the job. When selecting candidates for interview the employer is usually reasonably confident that the right candidate will be found in the group of five or six selected for the first round of interviews. The employer is primarily looking to fulfil three sets of criteria in their search for their new employee:

- *Can do* – the employer's primary aim is to find out if you the candidate can fulfil the duties of the job. Your skill levels, previous experience and achievements included on your CV/application form will have convinced the employer that you have these abilities and should be invited to the interview stage. When you reach the interview stage the employer's main role will be to probe into these skills and achievements in a little more detail to ensure a match between your skills and experience and the employer's requirements.

- *Will do* – we have all come across individuals in our working life who have the skills and abilities to do a job well, but for some reason fall short of the mark. It may be because they are lazy or do not have a real interest in the work they are doing, but whatever the reason they can become a liability to both their employers and their work colleagues. Part of the interview process is normally directed towards probing your achievements in the workplace – our achievements are what sets us apart from colleagues who do the same job and may have the same skills and background. Your previous achievements can highlight to an employer that you are an individual who will commit to the job and will do the tasks expected of you.

- *Will fit* – The employer will want to ensure that your personality and inter-personal skills are commensurate with the role and you will fit in with your colleagues. This is especially important if the job role involves fitting in with a team – it would be a costly mistake to introduce an individual into a working environment who did not suit the team personality or, even worse, caused resignations within an established team.

The three stages of *can do*, *will do* and *will fit* are equally important to you as a job hunter as they are to an employer. The interview is your opportunity to find out if the job role and the company are right for you. You may be confident that you have the skills and drive to do the job successfully but it is also vital to ensure that you are happy and that your personality will fit into the employer's environment.

Preparing for the interview

'Prior preparation prevents a poor performance.'

These are known as the 5 Ps. Remember them and apply the statement to every-thing you attempt to achieve in life. Very few of us can hold our hands up and say that we achieved a goal in life at the very first attempt and without preparation. If you are one of the lucky few, then well done, but the rest of us mere mortals have learned to our cost in the past that we need to prepare to succeed.

Approaching the job-hunting process and progressing through the stages requires preparation at every step of the way. The amount of effort you apply to preparing for an interview will directly affect your success rate and the eventual outcome of the whole process.

Preparing well for an interview will increase your chances of success and if you follow my seven steps you will gain an advantage over your fellow job hunters.

Seven steps to success

Preparing yourself

The first step in this whole process is to prepare yourself for interview. Remember that you have been selected for the interview because the employer believes, from the information you have provided so far, that you have the skills and experience to do the job. Banish the nerves you may feel and use the adrenalin surging around your body to your advantage. Remind yourself that you have the ability to do the job and of the reasons why you applied for the role in the first place. The interviewer will want you to do well in the interview; they are after all looking for their next employee and will get no satisfaction from interviewing an individual who looks as if the whole experience is making them ill, so be confident.

Dress for success

Imagine walking in to greet the interviewer. Before a word is even exchanged between you, you will very quickly and unconsciously form an opinion in your mind of them based on the way they look. This is known as non-verbal communication. As you size up the interviewer they will be simultaneously be carrying out the same exercise on you. Every time you meet someone new you will gain an initial impression of them within the first 15 seconds of meeting. As time passes our initial impressions may change as we get to know the person better; however, in an interview scenario these first impressions are vital and can make the difference between getting a job offer or not. In an interview scenario it is vital to dress to impress, since, by presenting the proper image to the interviewer, you are signalling to them that you will fit into their organisation by the way that you look.

I recall a situation many years ago when a colleague of mine was interviewing for a new member of staff. The candidate sailed through the initial interview, was dressed appropriately, communicated very effectively and seemed to have all the characteristics required for the demanding role. A second interview was duly arranged with my colleague's manager and the candidate invited along to an interview, which in normal circumstances would have been a mere formality. Before the candidate commenced any form of verbal communication she blew her chance of being offered the job by the first impression she created to the interviewer. She appeared for the interview in a skirt and blouse, bare legs and sandals – not a crime you would imagine on a very sunny day. However, she had shown a complete lack of understanding as to the requirements of the position, which had been clearly explained at the first interview. The primary role of the successful candidate would be to visit corporate clients. Imagine what impression she would create to a client of the business if she had shown up for an appointment dressed as she was.

The safest way to dress appropriately for an interview is to err on the side of caution. Unless specifically informed to the contrary you should always dress in a corporate manner. Remember that you do not know the personality of the interviewer and a more conservative dress sense is always the best policy. Another good idea is to observe prior to the interview the employees currently working at the business. How are they dressed? Follow their lead and show that you will fit in by what you wear. I am not suggesting that you should become a clone of the employer and lose your individuality but it is important to remind yourself that you are attempting to create the best possible impression during the interview. Do not stack the odds against yourself by rebelling. If the dress code is simply not you, then now would be a good time to ask yourself if this type of role is best suited to your personality.

Dressing well for interview will also give you added confidence. If you feel the part you should find it easier to portray the impression you want to leave the interviewer with – that you are right for the job.

For women I would suggest:

- a two-piece outfit in a traditional colour such as navy blue, dark grey or black. Avoid pinstripes or any other fabric which may draw unnecessary attention. A skirt and jacket suit is preferable to a trouser suit although these are perfectly acceptable in most organisations, and always ensure that the skirt length is just over the knee
- plain white or cream blouse with long sleeves
- black, brown or navy leather shoes with an appropriate heel size, freshly polished
- stockings or tights in a neutral colour
- matching handbag
- well-groomed hair
- subtle jewellery (earrings, wedding/engagement rings, small neck chain)
- subtle make-up.

For men I would suggest:

- a two-piece corporate business suit in a traditional colour such as navy blue, black or dark grey.
- plain white or blue shirt with long sleeves
- conservative tie (avoid novelty ties)
- freshly polished black or brown leather shoes
- black socks – non-patterned and definitely not novelty
- recently cut and well-groomed hair
- jewellery – only a wedding band and wristwatch.

Finally, now you are dressed for success, just a few other titbits of information to ensure that the first impression you create is the right one:

- Bathe or shower prior to the interview, turn up looking freshly laundered.
- Do not wear perfume or aftershave.
- Do not smoke at least one hour before your interview as the smell will linger.
- Do not drink alcohol at least 24 hours prior to the interview. It may affect the sharpness of your brain and manifest itself to the interviewer in the form of bloodshot eyes or bad breath.
- Ensure your nails are clipped and free from dirt, even if you work in a manual job.

Body language

Body language is the second tool in non-verbal communication. Your initial reaction to a person, as previously discussed, will start to form as soon as you see them for the first time. After the initial observation period has passed, the next stage builds on the first impressions by adding information from what an individual's action tell you – known as body language. In an interview scenario your body language will unconsciously help to guide the interviewer in assessing your suitability for the role.

Body language covers a multitude of behavioural practices but for the purpose of an interview scenario there are certain key characteristics to be aware of:

'People like people who are like them.'

I often use this quote when training candidates in the art of successful interviews. Basically what it means is that we are drawn to people who are like us, whether they are friends or colleagues, we tend to bond with other people who share similar characteristics to us. This is true in an interview situation where the interviewer will more likely bond and be predisposed to select candidates with whom they feel they have something in common.

Let's take a look at some body language communication and discuss what it might represent to an interviewer.

Eye contact

Maintaining a reasonable amount of eye contact with the interviewer will indicate that you are comfortable with the questions asked of you and are able to relate in a confident manner. If you feel slightly uncomfortable in maintaining eye contact a good trick is to focus your eyes just at the line of the interviewer's eyebrows. This will help take your mind off the need to maintain contact but will look to the interviewer as if you are.

Handshake

A good firm handshake again represents confidence and will give the interviewer an initial strong impression of you. The interviewer will normally initiate the handshake at the opening stage of the meeting and you should apply a firm even pressure, although do not attempt to go overboard and squeeze the offered hand too tightly. If you suffer from clammy hands then try to find something cold to cool your hand down, such as holding a glass of cold water.

Sitting position

Always sit up straight with both feet on the ground, hands should be placed in your lap as this will indicate to the interviewer that you are relaxed but confident. Try not to fidget with anything in your hands and be aware of any nervous traits you may have such as foot tapping or hand gesturing!

Smile

If you smile during the interview you will find it easier to relax and warm the interviewer towards you. Obviously, you don't want to come across grinning like a Cheshire cat – don't overdo it and try to make it as natural as possible.

Nodding head

Again all things in moderation! You want to make the interviewer like you and making encouraging signs like nodding will help you to move along the road to creating a bond between you and the interviewer.

Leaning forward

Subtle leaning towards the interviewer while listening or answering a question will help to show that you are interested and enthusiastic.

Mirroring is a tactic often used by experienced job hunters to adopt the poses and characteristics of the interviewer to increase their success rate at interview. Think back to earlier when we highlighted that individuals tend to stay within certain groups and pick people to work and be friends with who are like them. Mirroring is where we use clues left by the interviewer subconsciously to plant the idea in their mind that we are like them. It requires a great deal of subtlety to pull off but you can practise with your family and friends until you are happy that you have achieved the right level of balance. Imagine your interviewer displays some of the key characteristics just outlined such as smiling, leaning towards you when asking a question or nodding their head in response to your answers. It is as simple as storing this information when observing them and using it when you are communicating back; it is as easy as that. Try it out in some practice interviews with your friends and family without telling them what you are doing. Do you find that it makes you feel more at ease and confident? It works for some and not others. If it feels natural then use it, if not leave this tactic to one side until you have more interview experience.

By now you should be armed with enough information to present yourself well during the initial phase of the interview. It is vital to remember that what counts is how the interviewer will see you, so take off the blinkers and view yourself through someone else's eyes. Remember, non-verbal communication will provide the interviewer with a lot of information about you as an individual. By learning the key signals involved you can portray the best impression of yourself and convince the interviewer that you will fit into their organisation.

Prepare your knowledge

Before attending an interview it is vital to prepare your knowledge on the three most important factors governing this part of the job-hunting process:

- knowledge about your skills and achievements
- knowledge about the company
- knowledge about the job.

An interviewer will want to know why you feel that this role and company are right for you. A good interviewee will always be prepared and have gathered information to indicate that they have serious interest in finding out more about the opportunity. A poor interviewee will arrive badly prepared with little knowledge on either the job or the company and as such is much less likely to be considered a serious contender for the role.

Often all the data available on the job will be contained within a job advertisement or a job description. Your role as a serious job hunter is to read any information you have obtained very carefully and write down any questions you have about the role. These questions can then be used as part of the final stages of the interview to help you to build up a good picture of the role as well as indicating to the interviewer your level of interest in progressing to the next stage.

Compiling knowledge on the company is generally easier than it was due to the masses of information available over the internet. Most companies these days have a website that should provide you with a good knowledge of their products, market locations and other interesting information. For additional information and for research if the company does not have a website try logging on to newspaper websites, such as **www.guardian.co.uk**, where news archives going back several years can be found.

Prepare your answers

A good idea is to separate this section into two distinct areas, strengths and weaknesses. Interviewers normally concentrate on asking questions that are intended to highlight either a strength or a weakness, no matter how they word it or how well it is disguised. It is therefore wise to concentrate your preparation heavily in this area to ensure that you can predict to some degree the questions you are likely to face and the answers you would give. Lay your CV and details of the company such as job description, initial advertisement, company brochure etc. side by side and attempt to review the information you have, as if you were unconnected to the situation. What would the interviewer see? What strengths and weaknesses would they highlight?

Your weaknesses

Attempt to identify any areas in which you may have weaknesses and practise your responses to them (see further in Chapter 15). I am not attempting to heighten your anxiety levels by concentrating on your weaknesses the night before the interview, but everyone has areas they feel less confident about so it will lessen your anxiety if you are prepared. What is important is to be prepared for all eventualities and if you do have any weak areas you can bet that the interviewer will ask you about them. Practise how you would minimise and overcome any grey areas in your skills and experience and convince the interviewer that you are the right individual for the job. Remember back to the beginning of the chapter where we stated that you have been invited to the interview because the employer believes that you have the necessary skills to do the job. If you have weaknesses they will already have been spotted in your application and considered unimportant enough not to rule you out.

Your strengths

In the same way you reviewed your response to questions on your weaknesses, you should refresh your memory on the skills and experience that brought you to this stage in the job hunting cycle. Your strengths are the reasons why the employer has invited you along to the interview and they will want to discuss them. Think back to when you were compiling your CV and how difficult it was to extract some of the key information stored in your brain to enable you to write it down on a piece of paper. Some people find it equally difficult to relay information from their CV and communicate it verbally in an interview scenario. It is vital to reread your CV and talk out loud to yourself prior to the interview to reinforce your key selling points and implant the information into your brain in a clear and logical manner. If you practise talking out loud about your skills and achievements it will make it much easier for you to feel relaxed when asked questions about them and also enable you to provide well-thought-out and informative answers.

We will go into much more detail about this in Chapter 15, but for the time being practise talking about your strengths and weaknesses as if you were in an interview situation. Ask friends and family to help if you feel a little silly having a two-way conversation all by yourself! Remember – be objective and don't be tempted to elaborate on the truth.

Prepare your questions

A good interview should be rounded off with you asking a few well-thought-out questions about the company or the position. If you have conducted your research on the company and on the job, you should have thought of some key questions that would be particularly important to you during the decision-making process. The ultimate aim of asking questions at the end of an interview is to indicate to the employer that you are genuinely interested in the position and to give you the opportunity to find out if the organisation is right for you. Don't be tempted to ask questions just for the sake of asking, especially if the question has already been answered during the interview process, although it would, of course, be perfectly reasonable to clarify an answer you have already been given.

I would recommend preparing your questions while you are conducting your research on the company and taking them along with you to the interview. Only ask questions that directly relate to the role or the company. You should ask questions that show a real interest in the organisation and forward thinking on your behalf.

Do ask

1 How well the company has performed in relation to its major competitors over the past two years?
2 To whom would the position report directly?
3 What are the key challenges facing the department I would be part of?
4 How many people work for the same department?

5 What are the key skills and attributes needed to progress within the company?

6 What would be the immediate challenges faced in the position I am applying for?

7 Are regular performance appraisals carried out at the company?

8 What is the company growth plan over the next five years?

9 How many staff does the company currently employ? Have they any plans for expansion?

10 Why is the current position open? Has the previous incumbent been promoted, left the organisation etc.?

The types of question detailed here would provide the interviewer with a good indication that you were seriously interested in finding out more about the organisation and would help to create a lasting impression of a well-thought-out and prepared candidate. Try to limit your questions to three or four – you don't want to give the interviewer the impression that their information sharing was inadequate – and there will be plenty of time to ask more questions further down the interview process.

Equally, there are questions you should avoid. No matter how important they may seem to you, do not ask them at an interview. They will give the interviewer the wrong impression of what is important to you and could scupper your chances of progressing to the next stage.

Don't ask

1 What are the holidays?

2 Does the company pay sick pay?

3 What is the pay?

4 What is my boss like?

And don't:

1 Use first names or become overly familiar with the interviewer.

2 Smoke even if invited to do so.

3 Show anxiety.

4 Share your opinion on topical issues such as race relations, age discrimination, smoking and trade unions – in fact anything that may lead you into potential conflicting territory with the interviewer.

5   Look at your watch or display any signs of boredom.

6   Assume a submissive role – treat the interviewer as your equal, but with respect.

OK, so you should now have the tools and knowledge to do a great interview. Remember: be prepared, ask intelligent questions and stand out from the crowd!

Prepare your journey

Unless you are absolutely sure of the interview location and journey time it would be wise to undertake a practice run at least a couple of days beforehand. Preparing your journey will help to minimise any additional stress on the actual interview day if you know exactly where you are going and how long it takes to get there. I would suggest that you aim to arrive at the interview site at least 15 to 20 minutes prior to the interview to take care of any last-minute hitches with parking or public transport. It is easier to take a walk around the block to kill some time than arrive at the interview flustered and out of breath – or even worse, late!

Mental focus

Dealing with the nervous tension surrounding an interview is the norm for most of us, whether we are just starting out after leaving school/university or are progressing up the career ladder. Learning to relax in interviews is essential to ensure that you give the best possible impression of yourself to the interviewer. Remember back to earlier in the chapter where we discussed how the interviewer would feel if they interviewed a candidate who looked ill and uncomfortable during the whole process. Learning to relax is a technique that will help you to feel more comfortable about your own abilities and be better equipped to communicate fluently about your skills and achievements. When dealing with nervous candidates during my role as a career consultant I often ask them to put the interview in perspective, after all, what is the worst thing that can happen? They won't get asked to run around the block stark naked! The worst that can happen is they don't get the job, but at least the experience will help them to gain knowledge and improve on their interviewing techniques for the next time.

Some of you may already be familiar with combining relaxation techniques with mental imagery to focus on achieving your goals in life. It involves using mental imagery to set out your goals and objectives by placing the image of what you want to achieve at the forefront of your conscious mind.

Remember back to Chapter 1 of the book when we discussed the mental fine-tuning that athletes adopt to help them achieve their goals. Imagine the night before a big race, the athletes know that they have put the hard work into preparing for this race and mentally focus on powering up their mental and physical state to produce the best performance of their life. It doesn't matter to them if there are others in the field who have run faster times that year or who have beaten the athlete in every previous outing, what is important is to imagine crossing the finishing line ahead of these other athletes. Imagine how easy it would be for that athlete to let the self-doubt flood in with the knowledge that he has never beaten the other athletes he will be racing against. How effective do you think he would be in the race if he dwelled on these facts? What is important to remember is that the tools athletes use to boost their self-confidence and beliefs are available to all of us. It just depends whether or not you choose to use them.

Let's imagine that you use the same tools when preparing for a job interview that an athlete would use before a big race. Before we embark into your imagination, let's take a minute to practise the art of relaxing. There are many good books and tapes on the market designed to teach people the art of relaxation, especially if you have not consciously practised the techniques in the past. If it helps you can tape record your own voice and mentally prepare yourself for relaxation by listening to it on a personal stereo, that way you can focus on relaxing until the whole process becomes second nature to you. If you've never tried this technique before, then give it a shot, after all, what have you got to lose?

Imagine yourself arriving at the interview, you are dressed for success and feel confident about the image you will present to the interviewer. You can see yourself confidently shaking the interviewer's hand and following them to the interview room. Your brain is extremely sharp and because you are relaxed you find that you are comfortable discussing your skills and achievements with the interviewer. Each time you are asked a question you confidently relay your answer. You feel good and can see that the interviewer is impressed by your answers and overall presentation. You feel your body language has been subtle but you have managed to mirror the interviewer well and, all in all, your performance has been everything you would have wished it to be. You shake the offered hand of the interviewer and confidently leave the interview room, knowing that you have performed well at this interview.

Now imagine you could feel this confident and in control every time you felt yourself in a situation where, in fact, you felt ill at ease or nervous. Learning to relax is easy; it may take a few attempts to master, but bear with it because it really can make all the difference to how you come across in interview situations. Your mental imagery can help you to project the goal you want to achieve and doing well at that interview. You can prepare yourself for whatever hurdles are put in your way; you will overcome them and be first to cross that finishing line. Be confident!

Preparation checklist

At least one day before your interview I would suggest compiling an interview checklist to satisfy yourself that you have done all the necessary research required and can confidently approach your interview fully armed with knowledge about yourself and the job/company.

Preparation checklist	Completed
I have prepared what I am going to wear on the interview day and checked that it is presentable and appropriate	
I have reviewed the job advertisement/job description against my CV and I have a clear idea of how my strengths and weaknesses match up against the job requirements – I can relay this fluently	
I have thought about my achievements and where I made a difference to my previous employers	
I can speak about my skills and experience with fluency	
I have prepared a list of questions to ask at the end of the interview and I have them with me	
I have conducted all the background research on the company	
I have prepared my journey and aim to arrive at least 20 minutes early	
I have two copies of my CV with me together with the interview confirmation details	
I am confident about my abilities, I am relaxed and will do well	

Competency-based interviews

'Past behaviour is the best predictor of future performance.'

As previously discussed the ultimate aim of any job interview is for the employer to find out if you:

■ *can do* the job

■ *will do* the job

■ *will fit* into the organisation.

In order to predict these three key indicators a trained interviewer will often conduct what is known as a competency-based interview.

Competency interviewing normally encompasses behavioural and situational techniques. Behavioural versions are based on the premise that your past performance will indicate to an employer your future performance. Your examples will normally take the form of providing references to situations you encountered in the past, while situational versions are similar in that they will focus on your past but you will be asked to provide examples of where you would have approached the task differently with the lessons learnt from the experience.

In plain language this means that the interviewer will, in the case of behavioural questions, ask you to quantify your answers with actual events that occurred in the past and, in the case of situational questions, ask you to respond to specific problems that may occur in your line of work and identify the reasoning used to arrive at decisions made.

I am often asked whether it is possible to prepare for competency-based interviewing. Many would disagree with me, but I will stick my neck on the line and say that, *yes*, you can prepare. Ultimately, you cannot predict what questions you will be asked and unless informed beforehand you often have no clear idea of whether you are going to be faced with a trained interviewer or someone whose total experience has been the interviews they have faced on the other side of the desk. Even if you face an untrained interviewer you can apply the lessons learnt in this section of the book to highlight your behavioural and situational characteristics, allowing you to stand head and shoulders above your fellow interviewees. So, you *can* prepare for a competency-based interview. Here's how . . .

Ultimately, the employer is seeking to hire an individual who has all the key characteristics that they know make for a successful employee. They may have already conducted some research within their workplace and highlighted the key factors that set apart their great employees from their not so greats. These characteristics form the blueprint of what they would like to measure their future employees against and are often used in competency-based interviewing.

Careful company research and a good job description should arm you with the key data to use as part of your preparation. Read the internet website or company brochures carefully – what is that company's key selling point to their customers? What do they pride themselves on? What information does the job description provide you with? What are the key characteristics expected of the new employee? What skills and abilities would you need to display in the job? Just think about these types of question for a moment to get your brain moving into the right direction.

Competency-based interviewing will normally attempt to cover a maximum of five key areas of competency to be used during the interview process, depending on the demands of the role.

Decision making

Lead question

Tell me about the most difficult decision you have made in the last six months

Follow-on questions

What made the decision difficult?

What factors did you have to consider before coming to your decision?

What circumstances required you to make the decision?

What actions did you take?

What impact did your decision make on those around you?

In this type of question the interviewer is attempting to ascertain if the candidate in his/her managerial capacity is used to making decisions and, more importantly, if they have ever had to make what they would term a difficult decision. The leading question opens up the conversation and the follow-on questions allow the interviewer to probe the decision and its reasoning in more detail.

Positive indicators would show that the candidate had recognised that there was an issue that had to be dealt with and had considered their response to it prior to coming to a decision. They would have shown complete understanding of the factors involved and the impact of their decision on those around them.

Negative indicators would show a candidate who perhaps had reacted to the problem in a hasty and unprepared manner without taking time out fully to consider the consequences of their actions. Lack of consideration and forethought may indicate an autocratic or erratic leader who attempts to change how things are done without giving due consideration to proven methods and working practices.

Communication

Lead question

Describe a time when you had to overcome difficulty in communicating with an individual or team

Follow-on questions

What was the situation?

Where did the difficulty in communication arise?

What did you do to get your point across?

What was the outcome?

How did the individual or team respond after the event?

In this type of question the interviewer is attempting to ascertain if the candidate has proven communication skills as well as identifying their method and manner of communication.

The leading question sets the scene to highlight if the candidate considers that they have been faced with a difficulty in communication in the past. There is no reflection on the candidate if they have or have not been faced with a difficulty in the past, what is important is how they viewed it and their subsequent actions.

Positive indicators would show a complete understanding by the candidate of the message they were trying to convey and their understanding of where the difficulty lay. Their method of approach in overcoming the problem would be considered and their perception of the final outcome would show a great deal of understanding if faced with a similar difficulty in the future.

Negative indicators would show a candidate who had difficulty in understanding the reaction of the group or individual they were attempting to communicate with. They would also perhaps show a difficulty in communicating verbally or in writing with individuals who did not share their particular views and would perhaps display stubborn and unreasonable personality traits. They may be insensitive to people around them and find it difficult to consult others for advice.

Planning and organising

Lead question

Tell me about a situation in which you had to coordinate several people to achieve a given goal or task within the past 12 months

Follow-on questions

What circumstances surrounded your selection as leader of the group?

What steps did you take to coordinate and lead the group?

How did the group respond to you?

What tools did you use to measure the progress of the group?

What was the eventual outcome?

Wildcard question

How did you prepare for this interview?

In this type of question the interviewer is attempting to ascertain if the candidate in his/her managerial capacity has experience of leading groups in response to specific projects. The style of management is studied in this question as well as looking at the planning and organising skills.

Positive indicators would show that the candidate had thought through the objective of the project and had lead a team; someone who had a very clear vision of the steps required to achieve the objective. The candidate would show they had taken clear responsibility for the progress and eventual outcome of the project. Good planning skills would indicate that the candidate was able to work in a structured and methodical manner as well as adequately maintaining and driving management information.

Negative indicators would show a candidate who had not planned the process adequately prior to setting out on the project. They may have displayed a reactive approach to any hurdles faced along the way and perhaps been inflexible in modifying plans. The interviewer would look for any signs where the candidate was unwilling to take responsibility for the actions of their team in the delivery of the project.

Wildcard question

This type of question may be thrown in during the exploration of planning and organising to ascertain how well the candidate responds to a change of direction and to measure their responsiveness.

The best way to prepare for situational questions is to apply the same reasoning applied to your behavioural questions and come up with some thoughts on whether you would have done things differently or indeed how you would react if the same situation were presented in a different light. I suggest taking a look at the questions and answers provided in Chapter 15 to give you some guidance in the sorts of question interviewers are likely to ask together with suggested answers.

The main point to bear in mind when answering behavioural or situational questions is to remember to stay specific and remember the reason why the question was asked in the first place – the employer is looking to hear about an actual event and how you dealt with it in the case of behavioural questions and how you would deal with given specific situations posed by the interviewer in the case of situational questions. Don't be persuaded to waffle on and keep talking long after you have made your point. Nerves often have a habit of doing that to us – stay specific and you will keep the interviewer's interest.

If, after reading through the questions, you are having difficulty coming up with examples, remember that you can use circumstances that occurred outside work. Remember back to Chapter 2 where we looked at the compilation of a CV? Sally used her out-of-hours activity as leader of a Brownie pack to show potential employers that she was responsible and had experience in organising and supervision.

15 Interview questions and answers

As we previously discussed you will normally have no indication prior to an interview whether you are likely to be faced with a competent or an incompetent interviewer. Competent interviewers will have been trained in the art of interviewing and have a very clear plan in the type of interview they intend to conduct and have an objective behind each and every question they ask you. Incompetent interviewers, by way of contrast, will have normally gained their experience from sitting on the other side of the desk and may conduct the interview in a haphazard manner, leaving you with the feeling that you did not get a chance to project your skills and achievements in a satisfactory manner. The important thing to remember here is that if faced with a competent interviewer you can prepare yourself and if faced with an incompetent interviewer you can drive the interview in the right direction.

A competent interviewer will normally ask you questions based on seven key characteristic areas:

1   questions about you

2   questions about the job you are applying for

3   questions about your previous jobs

4   questions about your skills and experience

5   questions about your job search

6   questions about the company

7   questions about your future career.

Interviews will normally cover at least one question from each of these key areas to enable the interviewer to gain as full a picture as possible of you. The intensity and number of questions will largely depend on your answers and the requirements of the role, the level of responsibility and the depth of knowledge required.

Think back to the section on CVs where we identified that one of the secrets to progressing to the interview stage was to identify the language that the employer used to describe their ideal employee. No matter what the position or the company, all employers look for certain key characteristics in their employees.

Let's take a look at the types of words and expressions that employers seek to separate the indicators of the 'greats' and the 'not so greats'.

Sorting the 'great' from the 'not so greats'

About you

Do your answers suggest the following characteristics:

Drive	Determination	Motivation	Dedication
Communication	Leadership	Energy	Honesty and integrity

About your previous jobs

Do your answers suggest the following characteristics:

Past achievements	Compatibility	Team player	Manageability

About your skills and experience

Do your answers suggest the following characteristics:

Good subject knowledge	Fluency and understanding	Transferable skills	Confidence

About your job search

Do your answers suggest the following characteristics:

Preparation	Realistic expectations	Genuine desire	Understanding

About the company

Do your answers suggest the following characteristics:

Researched	Excited	Culture fit	Desire

About your future career

Do your answers suggest the following characteristics:

Forethought	Realistic	Personal growth	Ambition

Keep these thoughts in mind as we progress through some commonly asked interview questions. As the requirements of the job unfold remember to stress your appropriate key characteristics and keep quiet about your weak areas. If the interviewer wants to probe they will, but don't present them with the opportunity! At all times during the interview process remind yourself of the golden rule:

RELEVANCE — RELEVANCE — RELEVANCE

To be relevant is to keep the interviewer's interest and ensure that you hit the target with each and every question.

If you find that you get flustered or lose your trail of thought then take a deep breath and ask the interviewer to specify a particular part of the question in order to allow you to regroup your thoughts, for example:

When you asked about gross profit performance, did you specifically mean my individual performance or the team performance?

Just to be clear on my understanding, do you want me to break down the daily tasks I was involved in and explain my individual contribution?

A closer look at what to expect

Questions about you

Tell me about yourself

An open question that is often used to start an interview off and can be a giant hole for you to jump into! If you are asked this question, take a deep breath and remind yourself of why the interviewer is asking – to open up the interview. They do not want to sit and listen to you rattling on for 20 minutes about your career going back 20 years and your passion for fly fishing! The interviewer has ample opportunity during the interview to ask you questions in more detail and if they want to know any more at this stage they will ask.

Provide the interviewer with a brief summary of your personal details and current employment details, for example:

My name is Steven Brown, I am 32 years old and live in Newcastle. I am married to Tanya and have two children aged 5 and 3. I currently work at Smith and Brown Engineering as a project manager and have been there for the past 5 years.

How do you handle rejection?

This question tends to surface when you are being interviewed for a role that could involve daily rejection – such as sales. The interviewer wants to ascertain whether you see rejection on a personal level or as part of the role. If you have had experience of rejection in a previous role it would be wise to use it as an example as part of your answer, for example:

In my previous role as telesales advisor for Widgets Blinds I encountered rejection on a daily basis. My approach was to see it as part of the role and move on to the next call where my new customer may have a completely different response.

What do you consider to be your three greatest strengths?

Think of three major characteristics that you possess that you consider relevant to the role you are being interviewed for. Think back to when you compiled your CV and applied for this role, what adjectives did the employer use to describe their ideal person? For example:

My three greatest strengths would have to be my attention to detail displayed in my role as an auditor, my enthusiasm for my work and the adaptability I have shown within a fast moving environment.

What do you consider to be your three greatest weaknesses?

The flipside that often accompanies the previous question. Suffocate the desire to tell '*the truth the truth and nothing but the truth*'. Remember, you are attending a job interview, not confession, so you do not want to tell the interviewer all your bad habits. Everyone has weaknesses so don't be tempted to say that you can't think of any; the best approach is to come up with a maximum of two, which should satisfy the interviewer. The secret to answering this question and finishing on a positive note is to choose weaknesses that can also be turned into positives, for example:

I would say that I find it difficult to work with people who display a lacklustre approach to their work; I am aware of this weakness and attempting to resolve it.

This statement shows a weakness but for an employer it could display the kind of characteristics they would like to see in all their employees – after all, no employer likes to employ lazy workers!

Do you prefer working alone or as part of a group?

This question is usually asked because it relates directly to the job you are being interviewed for. Does the job require you to work alone or as part of team? Most employers like to have the best of both worlds here as the demands of the job could change over time, for example:

I am equally happy working alone or as part of a team. My previous roles have required me to work on projects requiring both skills and I have been equally efficient on both.

If pushed to answer either way then target your answer towards whichever is more relevant to the role, for example:

I am a real team player and get a buzz out of working with others and contributing to the success of the whole team.

Do you like routine tasks and regular hours?

Are you a creature of habit that likes regular hours and routine tasks? Your knowledge of the role and previous work experience should provide you with some guidance as to why the interviewer is asking the question. If you have just finished your education and looking for your first job the interviewer would be looking to ascertain how well you will adapt from a student's lifestyle to the demands of a responsible job. If you have indicated in the interview so far that you enjoy routine then the interviewer may simply be seeking confirmation. Your guidance here is to adapt your answer to the requirements of the job, for example:

I accept that every role carries with it a certain amount of routine in order to get the job done. As for regular hours I would expect to have an indication of my core hours but will work the hours that are necessary in order to fulfill the requirements of the role. While at university I worked regular hours in a part-time evening role to help pay my way through education.

What kind of people do you find it difficult to work with?

Very much like the weakness question – no one likes to work with lazy, slack colleagues, for example:

I find it difficult to work with people who are lazy and constantly complain about their work.

Can you give me an example of your ability to manage and supervise others?

This question would normally be asked because the position you are applying for involves managing other people. The interviewer is looking to hear about a specific example of when you managed or supervised others. If you are not in a managerial position currently then give an example from outside of the workplace, perhaps you lead a football team or supervise a Brownie pack, for example:

I currently supervise a team of six call centre advisors within the customer services division of Widgets Blinds. I am completely responsible for ensuring . . .

In my spare team I manage the local under-12s boys' football team. The role involves supervising training and providing motivation for up to 30 youngsters playing in the Edinburgh Focus League . . .

I see one of your hobbies is reading/films. What was the last book/film you read/saw? Tell me about it

This question is all about credibility; you have stated in your CV that your hobby is reading so the interviewer is clarifying your statement. Many people fly into a panic when this question surfaces because they can't think of a title or the author, it doesn't have to be the very last book you read – the interviewer won't know – just so long as it is a book/film that you can give a 30-second summary of if asked, for example:

I am currently reading The Lost Tribes of the Amazon *by John Slater. It follows a search for the . . .*

Do you consider yourself to be thoughtful and analytical or do you usually make up your mind fast? Give an example

The interviewer is attempting to ascertain how much thought you put into decisions you make. There is no right or wrong answer here, use your knowledge of the job and its demands to achieve the right balance in your answer. An employer may not necessarily want a plodder who takes forever to come to a decision or an individual who rushes into decisions they may regret later. In order to stay in the middle ground you could answer something like this:

I would consider myself a little bit of both, I put thought and planning into any decision I make while having an awareness of the timescales involved.

This job

What do you know about this position?

The interviewer may ask this question very early on in the interview to ascertain your level of knowledge about the job you are applying for, as well as gauging your understanding prior to embarking on their explanation. Say it as it is, in other words you may have been able to study a job description and pick out the key responsibilities to repeat to the interviewer or you may have very little information available to you. Do not attempt to elaborate, simply state the facts as you know them. It is far more likely that your research will have uncovered quantifiable information on the company as opposed to the job, unless you are applying for an internal position. Your answer could be something like this:

The position of accounts administrator within Smith and Jones Engineering includes complete accountability for the sales and purchase ledger, including weekly and monthly reconciliation. The position requires an individual with at least three years' experience in sales and purchase ledger with an minimum of an HNC in accounting.

What aspects of your previous job have prepared you for this type of role?

This is where you get the chance to use your knowledge of the job and tie in your key skills to ensure a match. If you have insufficient knowledge of the skills required for the role then turn the question around by asking the interviewer to clarify, for example:

▶ *In order for me to answer that question adequately I need a little more information from you, could you describe a typical day in this role?*

The interviewer will then provide you with the key pointers that they consider to be of high importance in the fulfillment of this role. Highlight where your skills and experience match against the role, remembering to use actual examples:

In my previous role my problem-solving skills were displayed when I was required . . .

I displayed outstanding interpersonal skills when . . .

Don't you think this job is above your level?

A competent interviewer may throw this stress question in during a comfortable phase of the interview or as part of a stress interview to gauge your reaction and see how you perform under pressure. Many people ruin their chances of success by reacting in a defensive or offensive manner and see the question as a personal insult rather than what it is – a question designed to test your mettle! As with any stress question, your answer will very much depend on what professional level you are at and your own personal circumstances. What is important is to remain calm and answer the question in a controlled and unflustered manner, for example:

I believe that six years' experience at senior accountant level within one of the fastest growing IT consultancies in the southwest has prepared me professionally and personally to move up to this role.

What interests you most about this job?

This is where you set out your stall in matching your skills and experience against the requirements of the role. If you have insufficient information on the job to enable a concise answer then ask the interviewer to tell you a little more about the day-to-day responsibilities of the role. Use the information that the interviewer gives you to match your key achievements against.

How does this job fit in with your career plans?

What are your career aspirations? The interviewer is attempting to find out what direction you see your career heading in and where this role/company will fit in with that plan. Successful organisations hold onto their best people by providing them with clear and achievable career paths. Your interviewer will want to ascertain if your career plans will fit in with the job you are applying for and the pathway the organization is able to offer. Come across as too ambitious or not ambitious enough and you may scare the company off. Use your common sense on this one and use your knowledge of the company and the information you have gleaned from the interview so far to guide you in the right direction. It is important to get the balance right between what you are seeking as an individual and what you believe the company can offer you. After all, it would be better to find out at interview stage that the company had no real ambition if it is important to you. For example:

I am consistently striving to increase my knowledge and skills and I believe that this position can offer me a real step up in terms of challenge and experience. I feel that my present career plans would be more than fulfilled by this role.

What would you most like to accomplish if you had this job?

Use the information that the interviewer has given you so far about the requirements of the role in order to answer this question well. If you have not had sufficient information to give a good answer then ask the interviewer for some more background on the critical aspects of the role and use that to guide you, for example:

During this interview we have discussed the importance of attention to detail and team development as being the cornerstones of the role. I would plan to conduct a detailed examination during the early days in the role to ascertain exactly why the team are under-performing and put an action plan into place to tackle the issues raised . . . My major accomplishments would be to reduce return levels by 80% within six months and put staff training courses into place within the first three months.

What things did you learn at university/college that could be useful in this job?

The interviewer wants to find out what 'life skills' you have rather than hearing about specific courses you have undertaken. Slant your answers towards the information you have gained so far about the job and where you feel your personality traits and experiences will fit in. For example:

During my studies I worked part-time at Asda Superstores and learnt the importance of attention to detail while working as part of the cash-handling team. It was my responsibility to ensure that the cash floats for the tills were made up and checked prior to the till operators taking responsibility. This ensured that the accounting function ran as smoothly as possible.

Or:

I chose to do a degree in mathematics because of the analytical element of the course. I learned during my studies that this was one of my great strengths.

What kind of individual do you think we are looking for to fill this role?

The interviewer is attempting to gauge your understanding of the position and to apply a slight stress element to the question to throw you off guard. By the time this question is asked you should have gained a good insight into the role and the desired personality type based on the facts you have gleaned from the interviewer. If not, turn the question around and ask for more information on the role in order to answer the question adequately. If you know the role requires an individual with strong attention to detail and a hands-on management style, then align your skills with the desired skills, for example:

I believe you are looking for an individual with strong attention to detail with a hands-on management style displayed within a FMCG environment. I have several years proven ability where my strong attention to detail and analytical style under my direction helped to develop the top performing sales team within my previous organisation.

How many hours a week do you feel it necessary to get this job done?

There is no right or wrong answer here, the interviewer is attempting to understand your approach to work rather than the number of hours you feel necessary to complete your duties. Take a moment to reflect on your knowledge of the role before diving into this question, for example if the position requires an individual with excellent planning skills it would not be wise to say that you regularly work late into the evening and weekends to keep on top of your work as that would indicate someone who is perhaps not organised. Try to play the midline, for example:

I would expect to put in whatever hours were necessary to get the job done, however I pride myself on my ability to plan and prioritise effectively.

What areas of your skills and experience would you need to brush up to enable you to do this job?

The interviewer is attempting to find out if you have any doubts about your ability to do the job. If you are applying for a role where you are already expected to have the skills and experience you do not want to indicate that you would need training. Beware of digging a hole for yourself when answering this question. Remind yourself that when you applied for this role you believed that you had the necessary skills and experience and so did the employer when inviting you for interview – apply that belief to your answer, for example:

I don't believe that there are any areas within my skills and experience that indicate gaps in my ability to do this job well.

Previous jobs

What do you consider to be your greatest achievement in your previous job?

Keep your answer directly related to something that you played a major part in; don't be tempted to take the glory for someone else's achievements in the hope that it might bolster your case. In order to make the greatest impact when relaying your achievement make it relevant to the role you are applying for, for example:

My greatest achievement at Smith and Brown Engineering was the design and delivery of a new working strategy across two sites in Scotland. I successfully communicated and implemented the directive which resulted in a net saving of £50K pa.
Or:
My greatest achievement during my career at Jeans & Co. was the quality assurance programme which I designed and trained all employees on, which resulted in a reduction in seconds to less than 1% pa.

What kind of pressures did you encounter in your previous job?

Every job carries a level of stress and pressure no matter whether you stock the shelves in your local supermarket or head the board of a multinational company. The interviewer is attempting to gauge what you would term 'pressure' or 'stress' and how you deal with it. Remember to keep your answer relevant and don't be tempted to give the interviewer a blow-by-blow account of the stresses and strains of your previous job. Keep your answer simple, for example:

My previous job carried a degree of pressure that I found stimulating and enjoyed working with. I was required to produce 500 units per day and found that working to these daily targets together with a tight quality schedule provided me with a sense of achievement.

Which particular aspect of your previous job did you find most frustrating?

This is not your chance to offload all your frustrations about your previous job to a friendly ear! The interviewer is attempting to find out if you have the desire to fit into the role based on your perception of your previous role. Everyone at some time or other finds aspects of their job frustrating, whether it be a lazy work colleague or incompetent boss. However, this information is for you to know and should not be shared with the interviewer. By the time you have reached this stage you will have done a great deal of thinking as to why you want to move jobs and come up with good reasons, for example:

I found that I had reached a level where I was not able to grow professionally and the company had no suitable positions available to enable me to take the next step.
Or:
The company was family owned and I often found that there were conflicting ideas on how the company should be run, which directly affected me.

The most important factor to remember here is that if you have to be critical of anything in your previous role ensure that your comments are constructive.

What particular aspect of your previous job did you find most rewarding?

This question normally accompanies the one on frustrations and is your opportunity to highlight the skills and experience you possess in line with the requirements of the job you are applying for, for example:

I enjoyed the challenges and pressures of the job. Dealing with customers every day over the telephone allowed me to develop my customer service skills and become one of the most successful credit controllers last year.

What areas did you feel your manager could have improved on?

This question is asked in a manner that assumes that you will have a critical opinion of your manager's skills and ability. No matter what job you are in or what country you live in, at least 90% of individuals regularly criticise their managers. Everyone at some time thinks that they could do a better job. That information is strictly for you and not for the interviewer! The interviewer is interested only in finding out if you may present manageability problems; they are not interviewing your manager for the position! No matter what your opinion do not be critical, for example:

Mrs Smith was an excellent manager and I learnt a great deal while working in her department. I do not feel that there are any areas she could have improved on.

▶   No matter what the interviewer says next, do not allow yourself to be drawn into divulging criticism – stick to your guns!

Can you think of a problem you encountered in your previous job and the steps you took to overcome it?

An interviewer normally asks this question because they want to follow your logic. How did you identify the problem and what did you do to resolve it? Try to make your answer relevant to the type of position you are applying for and show a logical trail of thought, for example:

In my role as sales manager I became aware that a manager from another division had been giving my team instructions which were contrary to my own. I arranged a meeting with him to communicate my concerns and find out why he felt it necessary to provide training to my team. The meeting was extremely constructive and I understood that he had only been trying to be helpful and had misunderstood his areas of responsibility.

Tell me about the last time you had to make a difficult decision in work. What made it difficult?

The interviewer is attempting to find out what kind of decisions you find it difficult to make. There is no doubt that most of the difficult decisions we have to make in our working environment involve people. Frustrations or problems encountered as part of our daily workload can usually be overcome and solutions found. Where a decision is difficult on a personal level but necessary on a business level is often a good way to answer this question. One of the most difficult decisions managers have to make is when they have to fire or make staff redundant. It is usually done with the interests of the business in mind but this does not make it any easier for the person making the decision; for example:

Recently I had to let one of my sales team go because of their inability to reach set targets. I had provided them with extra training during the previous six months and felt that I could do no more to help them. The decision was in the best interests of the business, but I still found the decision difficult because I knew the effect the sacking would have on his family.

For non-managerial positions, difficult decisions are often linked to delegation and liaising with our workmates, for example:

Recently I was tasked by my manager to complete a number of projects within a given timescale. I very quickly realised that it would be impossible for me to achieve the objectives in the time required. I had to go back to my manager with a request to prioritise the projects to ascertain their order of importance. It was a difficult decision for me to go back to my manager and ask for help, however, I decided that he needed to be aware of the situation as soon as possible and give guidance on a possible solution.

Did you achieve your targets last year? What were they?

This question will normally surface if you are applying for a job with a sales element and also in some senior management roles. It is asked as a direct question and always followed up by at least one further question intended to probe your achievements in greater detail. Don't view the question as stressful. If you have worked to targets and deadlines in the past then have your facts and figures at the ready, for example:

I achieved all my targets during the past 12 months. I had an individual target of £12,000 a month and achieved an average of £14,500 over the course of the year.

My annual target was to reduce staff turnover by at least 15% last year, I achieved an overall reduction of 25%.

If you haven't achieved your targets you may find the question uncomfortable and be tempted to elaborate on the truth. Give this question some thought prior to any interview situation in order to clarify in your own mind the reasons for your failure to achieve. There may be numerous viable reasons why your targets were not met and I would suggest concentrating on this rather than being untruthful or allowing your answer to focus on the negative aspects. End your answer on a positive, for example:

During my time at Smith and Brown Engineering I achieved my targets for the majority of the year. Market situations changed during the summer months and despite my hard work and effort I found that customers were simply not in a position to buy our products until later in the year. I evaluated my strategy and am happy to say that the situation was temporary and went on to improve greatly during the remainder of the year.

How would your team describe your style of management?

A deviation from the normal 'how would you describe your style of management'. The interviewer is asking you to view your style through the eyes of your team and is aware that they may have a very different opinion to how you view yourself. Be aware of the type of management traits the position requires and focus your answer towards that arena. Remember that your team is not here to voice their opinion so don't say anything that you may come to regret! For example:

My team would say that I am a firm but fair manager, who encourages and strives to keep open clear lines of communication in order to promote the self-development of my team.

You seem to have moved jobs frequently? Why is that?

Employers are wary of job hoppers and will ask this question at interview to delve into your reasoning behind job changes. You should attempt to show constructive reasons and give the interviewer some understanding of your reasons. If you have been guilty of job hopping in the past then you could show how you have learned from your experiences and now have a clear focus on where your career path lies, for example:

After leaving university I was unsure of exactly the type of job that would suit me and tried out various different roles before finding a job I really enjoyed. I have been a finance assistant for over two years now and have found my previous experiences to be useful in my current role.

Or:

I made the mistake in my two previous roles of focusing on my short-term objectives rather than where my career aspirations lay and with the benefit of hindsight I would have made different decisions.

Your skills and experience

Where do you specifically see your skills and experience fitting into this role?

Before you jump right into your answer take a moment to weigh up the key skills and experience that the job demands. Match up your skills and experience to highlight your achievements and show the interviewer that you will make a difference to their organisation. If you are aware of any particular issues that the company have that you believe you can solve then use these in your answer, for example:

In my previous roles where I have been tasked to set up new systems I have made an immediate impact and reduced running costs by an average of 15%.

You mentioned earlier in the interview the need for a cost-effective solution to staff turnover currently being experienced by the company. In my previous role I put a recruitment and retention programme into place that reduced turnover by 10% within the first year and produced an overall reduction of 32% by the end of the third year.

How would you like to see your skills and experience developing within this role?

Will the role fulfill your expectations? What are your career plans? It is important for both the interviewer and you to discover if your career aspirations will be fulfilled within this role. Remember to be relevant, stick to the next five years and don't drop any gems into the conversation about your desire to go off travelling. It is equally important for both parties to discover at this stage that mutual desires can be managed and fulfilled, for example:

I would welcome the opportunity to adapt my previous experience in accountancy within a manufacturing environment to learn about a different industry. I see the chance to use my skills within a service industry as a great opportunity to further my experience and provide me with the challenge I am seeking over the next few years.

As a recent university graduate I am looking forward to putting what I have learned into practice within a marketing company. I hope to develop my knowledge further and embark on a steep learning curve within a commercial organisation to enable me to become an integral part of your team.

What would you say if I said your skills and experience were way below the requirements of this role?

Watch out. It's another stress question designed to see how you react when put under pressure. It seems as though the interviewer is knocking your skills and experience and the hotheaded out there might see it as a personal insult and react defensively. If you take a look at the question again it states 'if I said'. The interviewer is testing your manageability. No matter what the subject the best way to approach this question is with another question directed at the interviewer, bearing in mind their reason for asking, for example:

I would ask what particular aspects of my skills and experience you felt were lacking and address each one of these areas with examples of where my skills and experiences matched your requirements. I would expect that after this discussion you would be left in no doubt about my ability to do this job.

Do you consider your career progress satisfactory to date?

The interviewer is attempting to ascertain how you view yourself and introducing a slight stress element in the question. If you have any gripes about past employers or managers this is normally when they will slip out. Don't allow yourself to go down that path and open a can of worms! Every one of us could look back at our careers and wish we had taken a different decision somewhere along the line, but remember that the aim of this interview is to be relevant and proceed on to the next stage. Try not to elaborate too much and keep your answer simple and straight to the point, for example:

> *I consider that my career progress to date has been extremely satisfactory and I have gained a great deal in terms of knowledge and experience.*

What steps have you taken to increase your skills and experience over the past five years?

The interviewer is attempting to ascertain if you are the type of individual who takes responsibility for their career progression and takes the necessary steps to encourage it. This question sits alongside the manageability issue as it has long been proven that individuals with a keen desire to do well and increase their skills base are usually easier to manage and promote. If you have undertaken any skills enhancement courses this would be the time to mention it, also take into account the skills and experiences you have learnt during the past five years in your previous job roles, for example:

I consider myself to have been on a learning curve over the past five years when I have greatly increased my skills and knowledge of network administration. During this time I have attended various training courses both through my previous company and through private study in my own spare time.

What kind of problems have people recently called on you to solve? Tell me what you devised

Are you a problem solver? Companies like to employ problem solvers. As employees they contribute a great deal and often have a part to play in increasing efficiency and so reducing costs. When others seek you out it indicates that you are a recognised problem solver and therefore an asset to any employer. No matter what your job there should be a time you can recall where the business faced a problem and needed a solution, perhaps you formed part of a team or were individually credited with providing a solution to that problem, for example:

Working as part of a production line I was required to polish and make aerospace engine blades ready for the next stage of production. The process was time consuming because the blades were held in place by clips that would often break during the process. I designed an instrument that secured the blades in place and increased efficiency by over 100% within one week of trialling.

How do you keep up with the latest news affecting your industry/profession?

How much interest do you take in your profession when you leave the workplace? If you have a genuine interest in what you do, the interviewer will expect you to keep up to date with the latest happenings in your industry. In most professions there is a trade magazine or internet website to share the latest gossip and news. If you don't keep up to date then start getting acquainted prior to your interview. Employers want to attract individuals who have a real desire to learn and take steps to keep abreast of the latest happenings to ensure that they are at the forefront of their industry. Imagine a doctor who hadn't read a copy of the recognised medical journal for their specialisation. Would you trust them to diagnose an illness correctly?

When judging the performance of your team, what factors do you take into account?

This question often rears its head when the position you are applying for holds management responsibilities. The interviewer is attempting to find out what type of manager you are. As with similar questions relating to your management style it is important to have listened carefully to the clues provided in the interview so far as well as taking into account the culture of the company. If you were being interviewed for an IT company then their management style would likely be very different from that of a corporate bank in central London. Look out for the clues and adjust your answer accordingly, for example:

The nature of the department I currently manage requires individuals to work to tight deadlines and often operating under a great deal of pressure. When conducting quarterly appraisals I take into account the particular demands of each job role during that period in order to give a fair assessment.

Describe what you determine to be the top priorities in your job performance

How well do you prioritise? Do you use your time effectively? This question is designed to provide the interviewer with clues as to where your top priorities lie. Be very careful when answering this question as a wrong answer could do damage to everything else good you produce in the interview.

If you were a payroll manager the interviewer would expect that ensuring the staff wages were processed by the deadline to be one of your top priorities. If you stated that it was typing the minutes of the finance office meeting then the interviewer would be right to be concerned!

About your job search

How long have you been looking for a new position?

If you are currently employed the answer is irrelevant as you are looking for the right role rather than rushing to find any position. If you are unemployed the answer becomes a lot more relevant. The longer you have been looking the more likely it is that the interviewer will presume that you have difficulty in getting a job. The right answer in this situation would be to point out any training courses you have been attending, voluntary work etc. in order to expand your experience in your search for the right role.

Employed – *I have only recently starting looking for a new position and have not set myself a particular timescale to work to. It is more important that I find the right position rather than how long it takes me to find it.*

Unemployed – *Since leaving Barrow and Storey Coal Merchants in July last year I decided to take some time out to identify my next career move. During that time I have attended some interviews as well as undertaking a series of training sessions to upgrade my skills and experience.*

How did you hear about this role?

Interviewers normally use this question to warm up the interviewee and relax both parties before the real interview commences. Your answer should be short, simple and straight to the point, don't be tempted to ramble if it is rather a long story – remember the reason the interviewer is asking the question. Perk up your answer with a firm reference to your level of interest to start the interview off on the right footing, for example:

I saw your advertisement in the London Evening Standard *and immediately knew that it was the type of position that would provide me with a challenge and a chance to further develop my skills.*

I have followed the progress of your company over the past few months after reading an article in the Guardian. *I was delighted when I spotted your advertisement last month and knew that your role would fit perfectly with my current skills and experience.*

Why haven't you found a new position before now?

A variation of the 'how long have you been looking' question. Emphasise to the interviewer that your next position is of more importance than the time it takes to find it, for example:

I consider it vital to find the right career move rather than simply settling for a 'job'. My career is extremely important to me and because of the amount of time spent in work I would rather spend the time finding the right company with the right opportunity.

Why do you want to leave your current job?

This question normally appears in some form during every interview as it provides the interviewer with sound evidence of your reasoning skills together with an insight as to why you are sitting in front of them. People have a multitude of different reasons for starting out on the job trail, but the important factor to consider here is how your reasons sound to another person. Don't open a can of worms by stating a reason and then showing that you haven't thought it through when probed. Stay on the safe side and pick a reason that shows the desire for professional or personal development that is currently unfulfilled, unreasonable travelling time, company or industry insecurity, for example:

> *I have reached as far as I can go within my present organisation, my skills and abilities are under-utilised and I feel that a move to a larger organisation would provide me with the challenge I am seeking.*
>
> *My company have recently relocated to Bristol city centre and my travelling time amounts to around 2–3 hours each day. I consider this unreasonably long and am seeking a position closer to home.*

How well do you get on with your boss?

What you think of other people and how you relate it will tell the interviewer a great deal about your manageability. The question comes in various disguises but no matter what your opinion of your boss you should always say that you got on very well with them. Any other answer will open up a great deal of discussion in an area that you really do not want in an interview – you are here to discuss you, not your boss! From my personal experience I would categorically state that if you criticise your boss in an interview you will not be invited to the next stage. Remember, be relevant and move the interviewer on to more interesting areas – about you, for example:

My boss and I had a good working relationship and I would say that we respected each other's individual skills and personal qualities.

What other positions have you applied for?

This question is a variation of several others, but ultimately the interviewer is seeking two different pieces of information:

- whether you are specifically interested in that role with that company
- whether they are in competition for your skills and experience.

Every interviewer likes to think that their company is special and may question your seriousness if you have applied for many different jobs. They also want to be sure that they have all the facts available to them when considering whether to progress you to the next stage. The best way to approach this question is to play your cards pretty close to your chest. It would be wise to remain pretty non-committal and give the impression that you want to ensure that your next move is the right one and do not believe in applying for jobs en masse. You could have applied for many jobs but the interviewer will not be aware of that information unless you disclose it and, to be honest, it has no real relevance on your suitability for the job. I would suggest giving the impression that this job is the only one you are considering at the moment. In other words make the employer feel special:

I have certainly looked around at the current jobs in the market that suit both my skills and career aspirations. At this stage your position is the only one of interest that fits both key areas.

Have you received any other job offers?

The self-assured job hunter may be tempted to brag when faced with this question about how many offers they have received and turned down, whether it is true or not, in the hope of seeming in demand. By the same token, you do not want to seem downtrodden and without a single job offer after months of looking. Play the middle ground here, if you have received job offers don't go overboard and be prepared to give your reasons for refusal if asked, ensuring that they have sound reasoning behind them. If you have not received any then sidestep the question and give the impression that you have not yet found the 'right role', for example:

I have received one or two offers since I started looking, however it is important to me that I join an organisation that will make the best use of my skills and abilities.

I have only very recently started job hunting and I am fully committed to seek out the 'right role'. I believe that it is vital to find an organisation that will make the best use of my skills and abilities.

What are you looking for from your next role?

Your chance once again to sell your abilities and key skills to the employer; pay particular attention to the information you have learned from your research of the company and the detail provided during the interview so far. Align your key skills with what the employer has said they are looking for in order to achieve a match with what the interviewer wants to hear, for example:

During my six years at Widgets & Co. I have developed a real understanding of network processing and enjoy the problem-solving aspects of the role. My communication and management skills have been finely tuned over the years and I now feel that I am ready to move to a more challenging position. My next role should combine my management and communication skills displayed within a larger environment, allowing me the opportunity for personal growth and development.

What sort of company would you like to work for?

Again your chance to align your answer to the information you have gleaned so far. Hopefully you are attending the interview after conducting your research on the company and finding that it was the sort of organisation you wished to work for, for example:

I want to work for a company that rates personal development high on the agenda.

I want to work for a company with an international presence.

I want to work for a company where I feel I can make a difference.

How does this company compare with others you have spoken to – in terms of money, opportunities etc.?

Again, a variation of 'what other positions have you applied for'. This question is asking you to compare this job directly with others and could be a potential hole for you to jump into. The best way to answer this question is in a non-committal manner. After all, no two jobs are the same, for example:

That is an interesting question. Ultimately no two jobs are the same in terms of salary and opportunities so I would have to say that this position is certainly very interesting and compares favourably with other similar roles.

Questions about the company

What do you know about this company?

The interviewer is attempting to gauge your level of interest in the role. Have you done your research? If not, it would beg the question how do you know you want to work here if you don't know anything about us!

A prepared interviewee will always conduct some research on the company prior to attending for interview, irrespective of how interesting the company seems. Remember the 5 Ps – **p**rior **p**reparation **p**revents a **p**oor **p**erformance!

Why do you think you would like to work for this company?

If you have done your research you should be able to recall the reasons why this company perked your interest enough to go along to an interview. Remember that the interviewer wants to hear about the research you have conducted, to indicate your preparation and also to obtain an insight into your reasoning behind why you feel this company is right for you, for example:

During my research of your company I was interested to note that you are a progressive forward-thinking organisation that believes in investing a great deal in your employees. Your company has an excellent reputation and on a personal level I believe that I would fit into your organisation and share your desire to become the No. 1 supplier.

Do you think this company has a good reputation?

This is a common stress question and will often be thrown in during a comfortable phase of the interview. To show any sign of wavering when deciding on your answer, whether you know about their reputation or not, is the kiss of death. Remember you are here to flatter and impress the interviewer in order to proceed to the next stage; always answer positively, for example:

During my research into your organisation I did not come across any information that indicated a bad reputation, in fact, quite the contrary, you seem to have a very good reputation.

What are the three most important factors about the next company you work for?

Again a variation of similar questions, ultimately the interviewer wants to hear the three most important things to you and mentally match them up against what their organisation can offer. You should attempt to align what you have learned already about the company to ensure a match, equally it is important to ensure that the company can offer you what you are looking for. Use your answer to match up against the company offerings or as a discussion tool to investigate whether they are right for you. Remember, don't burn your bridges, keep the conversation on your wants and desires very subtle if there are discrepancies. If you progress to the next stage, that is the time to set out your stall!

Do you know anyone who works for this company?

The guy you know from the pub, or your sister's boyfriend's cousin may be a great laugh and seem like a really good sort, but their employer may have an altogether different opinion of them. You will skirt with danger to say that you know someone who works for the company, as the interviewer will unconsciously place you at the same personal level as them just because you know them. Unless you have had to declare on your application form your relationship to current employees (councils and local government tend to favour this) state that you are not aware of anyone working for the company. By turning your reply into a 'not aware' answer you have not told any provable mistruths.

Do you prefer to work for a large or a small organisation?

Not a rocket science question, align your answer to the company you are being interviewed for. Most people tend to sit on the fence on this one unless they have a definite preference either way, for example:

I am equally happy working for a large or a small organisation, I do not have a preference either way. It is more important for me to enjoy working for the company and feel a part of the team.

How long would it take you to make a contribution to our company?

This question helps the interviewer to assess your listening skills. It would be wise to clarify the question and ask what specific area the interviewer is referring to, for example:

I would predict that I will make an immediate contribution to this company, but in order to allow me to provide you with specific examples could you indicate whether you are referring to a particular area of my expertise or personal qualities.

The interviewer should then provide you with a specific instance, for example, during the first three months, when you could answer:

During the first week or so I would predict I would be learning about your company culture and specific work projects, after which time when both I and the company were comfortable I would expect to start making a contribution with the skills and experiences you hired me for.

What do you think makes this company different from your previous companies?

Your chance to flatter the company and use the facts you have learned about it during research and the interview so far, for example:

The company has a higher profile than any of my previous companies, I am particularly impressed by the importance you assign to employee development and your proactive approach is a refreshing change.

When you joined your last company how did you get on with the other group members?

The interviewer is testing your social skills and your ability to integrate quickly into a group, particularly important if the role you are being interviewed for involves joining an established team. Your answer should always be positive and give the impression that you have will have no difficulty integrating into a close team, for example:

Naturally, at the outset, I felt a little nervous excitement about joining a team that was already well established. But they made me feel very welcome and I quickly felt at ease and able to contribute.

Questions about your future career

What kind of job do you see yourself holding five years from now?

This question is always a favourite and is intended to ascertain where your career objectives lie. Some people make a real hash of this question by informing the interviewer that they intend to be in *their* job. Embarrassing, tacky and not recommended as it may make the interviewer extremely uncomfortable with you and will not make the rest of the interview an easy ride. Don't attempt to be smart, answer the question honestly, for example:

Obviously, five years is a long time in anyone's career and things can change, however, based on my current knowledge I would like to think that I will have grown professionally and personally to enable me to have advanced my career and taken advantage of any opportunities along the way.

Who or what would you say in your life has influenced your career to date?

Perhaps you have someone from your past professional or personal life who inspired you? This question is often difficult to answer when put on the spot; the interviewer is attempting to gauge where you get your inspiration from. When I have been asked this question in the past I tend to give the following example:

> *During my working life I have been lucky enough to work with some very skilled people who were exceptionally good at certain aspects of their role. I identified what made them good at what they did and have tried to follow their examples.*

The interviewer may then lead you directly on to another question that asks you to describe one of these individuals and what it was about them that inspired you, so if you plan to use this example be sure to have an answer prepared.

Wildcard questions

Tell me a story?

This question is intended to see how quickly you can react to a change in circumstances and to test your analytical skills. The important factor to consider here is that you clarify what the interviewer wants to hear about and then embark on your story. To launch into a story about what you did last summer might be interesting for you, but is not exactly what the interviewer wants to hear about. Start by asking:

Do you want me to tell you a story about anything in particular?

If the story is about your professional life then slant it towards where your skills and experience made a difference to your employer, bearing in mind the position you are applying for and its relevance to this role.

If the story is about your personal life then slant it towards your ability to get on well with other people, staying clear of any dating game stories!

If the employer leaves the decision up to you then always tell a professional story and attempt to keep it interesting and no more than one minute long.

Do you see this pen? Sell it to me

Always a favourite on the sales circuit but this question has recently begun to surface over a wide range of other roles. Its primary intention is to ascertain how you react on your feet to an off-the-wall request and to test your communication skills when put on the spot. If you have a sales background you should have heard of features and benefits – features are what makes the product great but benefits are the things that customers buy. Tackle this question by asking a number of questions to your 'customer' to find out what they want, for example:

What sort of pen do you currently use? What in particular do you like about this pen?

Depending on your 'customer's' answers gently introduce the pen you are selling and point out the benefits of this pen aligning your answers towards what the 'customer' has already told you is important to them.

If you stick to this method you will achieve what the interviewer is looking for, namely clarification together with good communication and problem-solving skills.

On a scale of 1–10 how well do you think you are performing in this interview?

A stress question that often throws interviewees, especially when delivered several times during the interview. To be too high would seem arrogant; to be too low would suggest a self-esteem issue. The interviewer is not suggesting that you are doing badly which is normally the first thought on being asked this question, so stick in the safe zone and stay around 8 or 9 throughout the interview, no matter how well or badly you feel the interview is going. Remember it is a stress question and designed to see how you react – don't rise to the bait!

What salary are you seeking?

This is always a difficult question to be faced with. A competent interviewer will very rarely ask this question during an interview where the focus is on your skills, experience and personality; however an incompetent one normally does. If asked this question, you are put on the spot to a degree. I would suggest that you inform the interviewer, very much in the same way you would communicate the reference question that follows, that you would prefer to find out a little more about the position and ascertain whether the position is suited to both parties before committing yourself to a set salary amount.

Can we check your references?

This question often catches candidates off guard, although it is fairly common at the senior end of the scale. This is a stress question and designed to test the reaction of the candidate. The answer should always be:

Of course.

And quickly followed by:

I would like to keep matters confidential at this stage until we have progressed further along the process. When we reach a stage where both parties are interested in progressing to a job offer I would be more than happy to provide you with further details.

Don't be tempted to give out any reference details until you have received a firm job offer in writing and spoken to your references to provide them with details of the position. If the employer requires a reference prior to job offer stage then come to a compromise and provide details of a personal reference or a previous job where you completely trust the referee (never give out details of your current role).

What do you think of me as an interviewer?

Designed to throw you off guard, no matter what your opinion always flatter the interviewer, for example:

I have really enjoyed this interview so far and feel that you have asked me a range of questions that have highlighted my skills and experience.
Or:
I think you are an excellent interviewer and while I have found the interview tough at times, it has certainly got me thinking.

How did you manage to attend this interview while you are still employed?

Have you employed an underhand tactic or told lies to your present employer? If you have, forget about it and don't be tempted to tell the interviewer the truth – they are not really interested but just trying to put you under pressure. Always keep your answer short and sweet and do not be tempted to elaborate, for example:

I took some annual leave due to me, in order to attend this interview.

If I were to give you a personalised, signed blank cheque, what would you spend the money on?

A favourite on the sales circuit, the interviewer is attempting to find out what motivates you. Depending on what environment you are being interviewed for it would be wise to ask a clarifying question, for example:

Can I clarify that the cheque is made out in my name and is for me to spend on whatever I wish?

If the answer is affirmative then your answer could be anything you like from a top of the range sportscar to your own racehorse. The interviewer is looking for you to convey enthusiasm and desire.

On a warning note: If this question appears in a financial services environment be sure to ask a few more clarifying questions to ensure that you have all the information available to you. You would feel extremely foolish if the point of the question related to fraud and you had not adequately explored the circumstances surrounding the presentation of this cheque!

Do you plan to have children?

An illegal question that, in various guises, still makes an appearance for female interviewees and is almost always asked by an incompetent interviewer. Irrespective of your plans you can answer the question with a direct:

I have no plans at present to have children.

▶   The interviewer normally asks this question because they may be wary of employing someone who then takes off 12 months later on maternity leave. I would advocate that this is not your problem and brush off the question in as polite a manner as you can in order to move on to more interesting things – your career!

16 After the interview

How did I do?

After an interview it is important to analyse how well you think you performed and write it down. It will help you to be objective about your own performance as well as improving your interview techniques and providing valuable information when selected to return for a further interview with the company.

Compile the information as soon as possible after the interview, while it is still fresh in your mind and you can clearly recall key pieces of detail. Here's a sample interview analysis sheet for you to practise on.

Job title
Company
Date
Interviewer's name and job title
Did I arrive on time?
How long did the interview last?
Did I feel I had adequately prepared for the interview? If not, why not?
Did I get asked questions I had expected?
Which questions did I feel that I answered well? Give details
Which questions did I feel that I did not answer well? Give details
Could I have given better answers with more preparation?

Was I relaxed and aware of my own body language? Did I remember to smile?

Did I obtain all the information I wanted about the position and the company?

Did I feel that I had described my skills and achievements well in relation to the job?

My overall impression of how the interview went

What is the next stage of the process?

Outcome (complete when you are informed of the result of this interview)

Dos and don'ts of interview follow-up

After evaluating your interview it is a good idea to follow-up; don't just sit back and wait for the job offer. Consider the follow-up process as a strategic part of your job hunting; it could give you the edge you need to get the job offer over your fellow job hunters:

Do write individual follow-up letters to each of your interviewers within two days of the interview. This shows interest and will keep your name fresh in their minds. Refer to your interview notes and highlight your strengths to the employer, especially when you feel you did not get the opportunity to discuss them at interview. An example of a follow-up letter can be found at the end of the chapter.

Do obtain the correct titles and names of all the people who interviewed you, ideally from their business cards.

Do alert your references and provide them with details of the position to ensure that they have a good understanding of where your skills and achievements match up against the job you have applied for.

Do call the employer if you have not received any notification from them seven to ten days after the interview, to ask about the position. Remember that timescales can change due to circumstances outside the interviewer's control, so do continue to build rapport and sell your key skills and achievements during the call.

Do double check your spelling and grammar.

Don't worry about typed versus handwritten – both are equally acceptable in follow-up letters as long as your handwriting is legible!

Don't hassle or make any demands of the employer during your telephone call as it could undo all the good you achieved during the interview process.

Don't stop job hunting, even if you feel confident that you will get the job offer.

Don't burn your bridges if you are unsuccessful. Remain professional at all times – there will be other job offers and opportunities!

Sample interview follow-up letter

25 Brown Street
Wetherby
Yorkshire YB1 2LR

25 January 2001

Mr T Smith
Smith and Brown Engineering
10 Glebe Street
Wetherby YB2 2PP

Dear Mr Smith

Thank you for taking the time to discuss the position of administration secretary with me. After meeting with you and getting the opportunity to hear more about your plans for the future of Smith and Brown Engineering, I was certainly impressed.

I am convinced that my background and skills coincide well with your needs and in addition I can promise to bring the commitment and desire that are so important in a position such as this.

I look forward to hearing from you concerning your decision on the next stage of the hiring process and, once again, thank you for your time and consideration.

Yours sincerely

Holly Green

part four

dealing with
offers
and rejections

'The optimist sees opportunity in every danger; the pessimist sees danger in every opportunity.'

Winston Churchill

17 Job offers

Approaching the finishing line

In Chapter 1 we discussed the similarity between job hunting and a 110m-hurdle race; in order to cross that finishing line you have to tackle a series of hurdles to achieve your goal. You are almost there! You have almost reached the finishing line, in fact it is clearly in your sights but before you can be sure of achieving your desired result there are some final hurdles to consider. These hurdles are completely under your control and preparing for them will give you the edge over your fellow job hunters.

Evaluating the job offer

Congratulations, you've received a job offer and all the hard work you have put into the process of job hunting has paid off. Now take a deep breath and prepare yourself for the challenges ahead. You have already experienced a range of emotions during the job-hunting cycle and the point when you finally receive an offer will be no different. Many people caught up in the momentum of job hunting suffer from unexpected emotions once the offer is finally received:

- Is the job really the one they want?
- Is it better than the job they have currently got?
- Is the salary offer as good as they expected?
- How are they going to tell their boss?
- How will their boss react?
- What if they are making a mistake?

If you are experiencing any of these job-offer demons, don't panic, you are not alone and it is likely that many of your friends and family will have experienced exactly the same feelings when faced with a similar situation. It is important at this stage to control your demons and focus on the path that led you to this stage of the cycle in the first place. Think back to Part 1 where we discussed the reasons why people make the decision to look for a new job in the first place, remind yourself of your motivating factors. Concentrate on these factors and use them to focus on the positives that will come out of changing jobs instead of dwelling on the negatives. Don't let your fears of the unknown unravel everything you have achieved up to this point and all the hard work you have put into getting here in the first place. Imagine yourself already in your new job; think of all the changes you are making and how your life will be improved by the opportunities it will present you with.

The hard work you have put into preparing for this role from the initial application phase through to the interview stage should have provided you with adequate information on the job and the company and, more importantly, whether it is right for you. It is important at this stage to reaffirm the information available to you, especially if you are likely to receive a counteroffer from your current employer. A cold hard look at the facts in front of you will help you to set your mind straight on the reasons why this role is the right/wrong one for you.

Job content

Is the content of the job interesting to you? Bear in mind that it takes the average person anywhere between six weeks and six months to master the day-to-day tasks of a job role. Does the role fit into your long-term plans; will it help you to develop your knowledge and experience?

Your supervisor

Have you met your supervisor? Do you think that you can get along with this person? Don't dismiss the importance of this question as discontent with a supervisor is one of the main reasons why people look to change jobs. You will want to work for a supervisor who has the ability to teach you new skills and help to expand your knowledge further, as well as showing an interest in your growth and development.

Your salary and benefits

Is the salary offered what you expected? Is it in line with the going market rate? If not, do you know why? When is your next salary review? Can you expect bonus payments, when are they paid and how are they calculated?

Location

Is the location right? Have you considered the travelling implications in terms of cost and time? Do you have to relocate? What other issues do you have to consider in terms of spouse's job, schools etc.?

Your co-workers

Have you met any of your co-workers? Do they seem the type of people you could work alongside?

Typical working week

What does the typical working week consist of? How many hours are you likely to work? What other commitments do you have outside work that may be affected by your working hours?

Company culture

Is the culture of the company suited to your personality? Is the company flexible or do they work to a very strict set of rules? How will the position alter your current lifestyle?

During my years of experience in helping people to find work I have found that this final stage is often the one key area that is overlooked in terms of its importance to the job hunter. The excitement together with the stresses and strains of looking for and finding the right job are heavily weighted against success unless you consider all angles and ask yourself the right questions at every stage of the process. An employer's and recruitment consultant's nightmare is the individual who does not focus on what is important to them until the offer is on the table. No one benefits from an unhappy employee therefore it is vital to reconsider why you wanted a change in the first place and what this position can offer you.

Compare accepting a new job with finding a new place to live in. When you first put your old house on the market you will normally have compiled a list of reasons in your head why you want to move – these could range from location to a desire for a larger property. As you start to progress along the house-moving chain you will normally view a variety of homes considered suitable for your needs. It is unusual to get a property with every single thing on your checklist but as you continue viewing you will eventually size up in your mind the things that are most important to you. Finding a new job is exactly the same; you start out with a list of your most important things which may number nine or ten, but as you progress you normally cut this down to three or four achievable key factors together with an accompanying number of added extras that make the job desirable.

By now you should have come to a decision on whether this job is the right one for you. Hopefully, your research prior to this phase and the thought put into the evaluation process have served only to confirm your belief that the role *is* the right one for you. Every decision we make in life involves some element of risk and without taking calculated risks it is unlikely that your career will progress in the manner you expect it to. Be brave and take the first step!

If, however, you have come to the decision that the job is not the right move for you then take some time out to revisit the earlier stages in the job-hunting cycle and find out where you went wrong:

- What factors did you not consider?
- How can you prevent this scenario happening again?
- Are your expectations realistic?
- Are you simply suffering from cold feet?

Offer methods

An employer or recruitment agency is likely to make the offer of employment to you using one of the following methods.

By telephone

If you are made an offer by telephone then you are likely to face the same distractions outlined in the chapter on telephone interviews such as a loud TV, barking dogs or noisy children! Take a moment to compose yourself and get away from any distractions in order to focus on the detail the employer/agency is imparting. Remember the importance of your voice when communicating by telephone; it is the only indicator that the employer/agency can use to judge your reaction to the offer. No matter what your decision it is always wise to sound enthusiastic and watch out for any negative indicators that you may unintentionally display, such as disappointment about a particular part of the offer. The job offer phase is your only real chance for negotiation and I would recommend asking for a reasonable length of time (normally 24 to 48 hours) to consider the offer.

By letter

If you receive a job offer by letter the employer/agency will normally expect you to make contact with them within 48 hours, which will give you ample time to weigh up the pros and cons of the position.

At interview

If you receive a job offer at the interview stage then resort back to the tactics explained during the telephone/letter offer section. Give yourself time to think and agree on a response timescale with the employer.

Offer negotiation

Irrespective of the situation in which you receive the offer, it is vital to ensure that you give yourself time to evaluate it prior to accepting or turning down the role. A good night's sleep can make all the difference when it comes to making a decision! It may be that the offer has everything that you wished for in terms of salary, bonus, location – and if this is the case then well done. Negotiation should only be used when you are in a position of power and it is important to get your ground rules firmly set before you move into this arena. The first question to ask yourself is how important the area you wish to negotiate is to your future job satisfaction. If you consider it important enough to sway whether or not you accept the job then you really have nothing to lose by asking the employer – after all, the worst that can happen is that they say no! Equally, if you don't ask you may well start a new job already carrying some resentment that could grow as the months pass and you start to settle into your new environment.

Common negotiations

- Salary
- Salary review dates
- Benefits
- Holiday entitlement.

It is important to remember at this stage of the process that this is one of the few occasions when you possess some real bargaining power and can use it to get the best possible deal. It is also equally important to evaluate exactly what you aim to ask for and whether or not it is realistic, for example if you are a school leaver and wish to obtain a further £2,000 on top of the offered salary, ask yourself what you have got to use as a bargaining chip. Probably very little, as the company will not benefit from your previous experience and your achievements are less likely to be of direct use to an employer. Contrariwise, if you are an experienced IT sales consultant who is currently producing revenue in the top 10% of your market, you could use your skills and achievements to prove to the employer that you are worth a little more than you are currently being offered. The key factor here is to be realistic about your expectations, then evaluate how far they are from the original offer.

Accepting/declining the offer

Accepting the offer

Verbally confirm your acceptance of the offer and follow up with a written letter of confirmation, which reiterates the job title, salary, start date and any benefits applicable to the post. Ask the employer to confirm your offer of employment together with salary and benefits in writing and state that you are looking forward to joining the organisation. See the section later in this chapter on resigning from your current role – don't be tempted to do anything else at this stage until you have a firm offer in writing from your future employer.

Declining the offer

Verbally decline the offer and follow up with a written letter confirming your decision. Be sure not to burn any bridges and thank the employer for their consideration to date. Explain in brief terms that the offer did not match your needs/expectations at this time but reaffirm your appreciation of the opportunity of an interview at that organisation.

Hedging your bets

Some people choose to hedge their bets by accepting one job offer while waiting on the outcome of another. Although this has very obvious benefits for the job hunter I would recommend against it based on the impression it gives of your ethical/professional conduct. You never know who you may encounter in your future career and behaviour of this sort tends not to be easily forgotten. Make your decision an honest one and you can hold your head up high.

Preparing to resign

By the time you reach this stage of the job-hunting cycle you should have received and accepted your job offer in writing and have a confirmed start date with your new employer. If you have not received an offer in writing for whatever reason, do not, repeat *do not* resign from your current role until you do.

You can expect to experience a change in how your co-workers and supervisor relate to you as soon as you submit your resignation so it is wise to prepare yourself.

As soon as you submit your resignation your employer will be watching you with a close eye, especially if your notice period extends to two weeks or more. I would recommend that prior to resigning you take some precautions to gather or remove any personal files from your computer or workspace, especially those that could be used against you. When removing personal items prior to your resignation, take care to do so in a subtle manner so as to not arouse any suspicion. Your method and manner of resignation should stay under your control for as long as possible.

Some companies have a policy in place that requires you to be removed from your office immediately. Your indicator on whether this is likely to happen to you should be when colleagues have resigned in the past – how have they been treated?

The resignation meeting

Approach your boss directly, preferably in his or her office and always privately. No matter what your reasons are for resigning from your job it is important to keep a cool head and behave in a courteous and professional manner. Many people use the resignation letter or meeting to air all their grievances – bad idea! It may make you feel better in the short term but could have future implications on your references or final salary, so whatever your reasons keep them short, simple and professional.

Prepare for your resignation meeting by writing your letter (examples are provided at the end of this chapter) bearing in mind that it should be short, sweet and straight to the point. Consider what information you feel is necessary to share with your boss during the meeting. It is to your advantage to play your cards close to your chest and impart as little information as possible about your new role, especially when your boss may be tempted to slander your future company and put doubt into your mind about the merits of your decision. Some unscrupulous bosses have even been known to attempt to destroy a job offer before a candidate has started! Play it safe and don't take any chances you don't need to.

Hand your boss the letter accompanied by a short statement such as, 'After a great deal of consideration I have decided to resign my position' and let them take it from there. It is advantageous to you to remain friendly and polite during the resignation interview, no matter how hostile your boss may become.

Dealing with counteroffers

A counteroffer is simply an inducement from your current employer to get you to stay with them after you've announced your intention to take another job. Mention of a true offer carries an actual intention to quit and is often the time when your boss will make you a counteroffer to persuade you to stay.

How do most people feel when a counteroffer is made:

- flattered?
- wanted?
- important?

Do not be fooled! In all my experiences I have only seen a few very isolated incidents where a counteroffer proved to be of benefit to the employee – accepting is tantamount to career suicide. In order to understand the emotion of counteroffers it is wise to take a step back and consider the situation from the employer's point of view; what are the likely thoughts that the employer encounters when a member of their staff announces their decision to resign?

■ 'I have only just got the department functioning at full complement, this means I will have to recruit again.'

■ 'I am going on holiday next month and this will really muck things up for me.'

■ 'This resignation will wreak havoc on the morale of the department.'

■ 'This couldn't happen at a worse time with the project to run.'

■ 'This is one of my best people; the resignation will directly affect the whole department.'

■ 'My review is coming up next month and this resignation will not look good.'

Whatever your employer's reaction or reasoning it is wise to consider that a counteroffer is very rarely made for the good of the employee! Whenever an employee resigns, irrespective of the reasoning behind it, it is a direct reflection on the boss and their gut reaction in most cases is to persuade you to stay until they can regain control of the situation.

While your boss is mentally summarising the effects your resignation will have on the company and, more importantly, on them at a personal level, their response to you will normally sound something like this:

■ 'We have plans for you scheduled to take place next month. I should have told you about them before now.'

■ 'We'll match the offer; your raise was supposed to take effect next quarter but because of your great service I will bring it forward to next month.'

■ 'You're going to work for who? I've heard bad things about them.'

■ 'I'm really shocked, I thought you were happy here, what can I do to persuade you to stay?'

■ 'You've picked a fine time to land this on me. Who is going to finish the project?'

Before you are swept along by the tide of flattery and emotion surrounding a counteroffer take time to consider the following important factors:

■ Counteroffers are only made in response to a direct threat to quit. Will you have to consider this approach every time you deserve a rise in salary or better working conditions?

- Your reasons for leaving and embarking on the job-hunting cycle still exist; conditions may seem more tolerable in the short term but will they really improve your satisfaction levels over the long term?

- Counteroffers are usually nothing more than stalling devices to give your employer time to replace you – at a timescale to suit them!

- No matter what the company says when making its counteroffer, you will always be considered a risk – it's human nature. Having once demonstrated your lack of loyalty to them your status in the organisation will diminish.

If you expect to receive a counteroffer, how should you deal with it? The easiest method is not to allow a counteroffer discussion to take place. If you give any indication to your employer that you may be susceptible to a counteroffer they may, using their knowledge of your personality, try to push the right buttons by focusing in on your areas of weakness to persuade you to stay with them. It is important, prior to any resignation discussion, to consider that a counteroffer may be made and mentally to prepare yourself to ward it off. By entering into counteroffer territory you will make the whole process of changing jobs a much harder one that it needs to be, not to mention the wasted investment of your and your present company's time and energy.

It is a natural emotion to avoid change and minimise disruption and for this reason many people fall into the trap of feeling guilty and find it hard to say 'no' to their employer when entering the counteroffer phase. Remind yourself why you have chosen to resign and stay strong and committed to your decision. You are making this move for the good of your career and your future. No one is indispensable and your employer will get along fine without you.

Resignation letters

Resignation letters come in a variety of guises but the most important factor to consider is to keep it simple. As previously discussed do not be attempted to put anything down in writing that you may later come to regret, especially when you require references or have a final salary to come. While writing and submitting a resignation letter may be an unpleasant task there really is nothing to it. There is no need to go into great detail about your reasons for leaving as these may be open to misinterpretation and could lead to difficulty when your references are applied for, for example:

While I enjoyed the job at Smith and Brown Engineering I found that my daily tasks had become repetitive.

This could easily end up in a verbal or written reference as:

Janet Smith was easily bored by repetitive tasks.

It is sufficient simply to state that you are submitting your resignation with effect from x and intend your final date of employment to be x (normally two weeks in advance or as stated on your contract of employment).

25 Glebe Street
Manchester M2 5BB

Mr P Brown
Smith and Brown Engineering
22 Brown St
Manchester M2 4LL

16 November 2002

Dear Mr Brown

This letter is formally to give notice of my resignation from Brown and Smith Engineering with effect from 16 November 2002.

My last day of employment will be 30 November 2002.

Please let me know if there is anything I can do to ensure a smooth handover of duties during my final two weeks with the company.

Yours sincerely

(Your signature)

18 | Dealing with rejection

> 'Nothing can stop the man with the right mental attitude from achieving his goal; nothing on earth can help the man with the wrong mental attitude.'
>
> **Thomas Jefferson**

I didn't get an interview / I didn't get the job – what next?

The process of applying for jobs and attending interviews can be both time-consuming and emotionally draining for the job hunter. You may have set all of your sights on a particular job and already be imagining yourself fulfilling the duties of the role, only to receive a rejection for interview or be turned down after interview. It is a natural emotion at this stage to lapse into negativity and allow yourself to wallow in self-pity, imagining that you will never get the job you want.

Remember back to Chapter 1 where we discussed the mental strength of athletes who continually push themselves toward the achievement of their goal? How many of them would be successful if they allowed every setback to interfere with their training regime or desire to win? None! Treat your job hunting in exactly the same manner: continuing self-confidence is an essential requirement for every serious job hunter to ensure that the desired amount of effort is put into each and every job application and interview – feeling sorry for yourself and allowing self-pity to take over will not help you to succeed and take you in the direction you want to go.

When receiving a rejection letter, or indeed no response at all, at the pre-interview stage it is natural to feel slightly aggrieved. After all, how can the employer reject you when they haven't even met you? Review your CV against the original job advertisement and attempt to see where your skills did not match up against what the employer asked for. Remember that the employer or agency may be deliberately vague in the advertisement in order to attract applications from the widest possible audience and you may not have been privy to all the information!

When receiving a negative outcome at the interview stage it is important to re-evaluate your performance and preparation. Look back at the notes you compiled after the interview and see if there are any indicators of where you might have prepared better. Perhaps you felt nervous and unable to communicate fluently? It is also equally likely that you did absolutely nothing wrong in the interview and you just were not the person the employer was looking for.

Remember that the employer has a mental check list containing three key pieces of detail when selecting new recruits:

- Can they do the job?
- Will they do the job?
- Will they fit in?

The employer will have selected candidates for interview based on the skills, experiences and achievements outlined in their CVs, providing a guideline for the *can do* and *will do* elements of their requirement. The employer will approach the interview process by further investigating these two elements and scoring your responses to their questions by matching them against their perceived requirements. The one element where you have very little control is the *will fit* as this is the sector on which most hiring decisions are based and it comes down to a simple yes or no: do you or do you not fit into the image the employer has of their new recruit?

Prior to having any form of communication with you, bar the initial viewing of your CV, the employer is likely to have a picture in their mind of the ideal individual for the role. The ideal individual's characteristics are likely to be based on the previous experiences of the employer when recruiting staff;perhaps they want to emulate a particular type of individual who has been especially successful or avoid other characteristics of an individual who has not been successful. Whatever the reasoning behind the employer's mental picture of the ideal new recruit, one simple fact remains – you are who you are and cannot change major parts of your personality to suit the particular nuances of an employer.

As long as you can put your hand on your heart and say that you produced a CV that was targeted specifically towards that job, as well as completing the seven steps to interview success, then it is just a matter of accepting that, for whatever reason, the employer did not consider you suitable for the role.

The most important step to take next is to move on from the situation and identify the positive aspects of your job-hunting experience so far:

- what you did well
- what you could have done better
- what you have learned about yourself
- what you will do differently next time.

Count all the skills and effort you have put into the process so far as a learning curve of experience towards getting the job that is right for you.

'The price of success is hard work, dedication to the job at hand, and the determination that, whether we win or lose, we have applied the best of ourselves to the task at hand.'

Vince Lombardi

Index